BLITZKRIEG

THE UNPUBLISHED PHOTOGRAPHS 1939–1942

BLITZKRIEG

THE UNPUBLISHED PHOTOGRAPHS 1939–1942

BROWN BOOKS

© Amber Books Limited 2002

ISBN 1 897884 87 7

British Library Cataloguing in Publication Data
A CIP catalogue record for this book is available from the British Library

Published by Brown Books Ltd,
an imprint of Amber Books Ltd,
Bradley's Close,
74–77 White Lion Street,
London N1 9PF

Project Editor: Charles Catton
Editor: Helen Wilson
Design: Hawes Design

Printed and bound in Italy by: Eurolitho S.p.A., Cesano Boscone (MI)

Picture credits
All photographs Ian Baxter/History in the Making

Contents

CHAPTER ONE

Germany Reborn

Hitler's Pre-war Gambles

Adolf Hitler had a clear idea of how he intended to achieve his political and military ambitions when he assumed leadership of the Nazi Party in January 1933. Revision of the Treaty of Versailles was paramount, along with German re-armament. Accordingly, he proceeded, over the next two years, to rearm and develop his army secretly in such a way as to avoid any preventive military action against Germany by the Versailles powers. The German Army was ordered to treble its strength from 100,000 to 300,000 men by October 1934. The German Navy began a new shipbuilding programme. The Luftwaffe began to design warplanes. Military pilots began to train under the camouflage of the League for Air Sports.

By January 1935, the German armed forces were expanding quickly and the Reich Air Ministry was intensifying aircraft production. In mid–March, compulsory conscription was introduced, and by the autumn of 1936, the Army had expanded to 36 infantry and 3 armoured divisions. It was through the successful trials of these armoured formations on manoeuvres that Hitler and the Army leadership were convinced of the value of this new weapon of war. The use of armoured formations was increased, and infantry divisions were reorganized into motorized divisions to expand operational and tactical mobility. Hitler ensured that a significant increase in armoured and motorized units would be available to the Army for 'offensively conducted defence' or for 'ambitious [or extended] targets'.

REOCCUPATION OF THE RHINELAND

Hitler decided it was time to utilize this increased German military strength for the seizure of the demilitarized Rhineland. The conditions of the 1919 peace settlement

LEFT: A column of vehicles queue on a road in southern Germany to cross over the Austrian border before *Anschluss* with Austria. Queues on the border stretched for 3.2km (2 miles).
FAR LEFT: Various motorcycles, armoured and unarmoured vehicles and personnel carriers from the 20th Motorized Division pass through an Austrian town, following the division's standard bearer, in early October 1938.

prohibited the German Reich from erecting fortifications, stationing troops, or undertaking any military preparations in the area which encompassed all German territory west of the Rhine, and included a 56.3km (35 mile) strip east of the river, incorporating the major cities of Bonn, Cologne, and Düsseldorf.

To Hitler, the current status of the demilitarized Rhineland was intolerable, and he was determined to reoccupy the zone, even with the likely prospect of military retaliation by France or Britain. It was a bold risk but a risk Hitler was intent on taking. In March 1936, with no more than 30,000 regular soldiers augmented by units of the *Landespolizei*, the hopelessly ill-supported troops approached the Hohenzollern Bridge in Cologne to begin what was called Operation 'Winter Exercise'. As the soldiers marched across the bridge they received a delirious reception from thousands of thronging crowds that strewed the way with flowers and paper chains. Eighteen years earlier, dejected columns of German troops had crossed this bridge following their defeat on the Western Front. Now they were back, this time to the fervent cheers of a welcoming country. Only 3 of the 19 infantry divisions crossed the Rhine that day, with orders to stage a fighting withdrawal if challenged by the might of the French Army. But neither the French nor their British allies seriously considered taking military action.

Hitler's gamble had paid off. His taste for further ambitious territorial expansion in Europe began to fester in his malevolent mind. His eyes were now firmly fixed on his next goal: the annexation of Austria.

ANSCHLUSS WITH AUSTRIA

To Hitler, Austria's entire history had been an essential and inseparable part of German history. As with the Rhineland, he believed Britain and France would not take military action to stop his crusade, but he still needed to increase the momentum of planning a military occupation without taking undue risks. The Austrian Chancellor Kurt Schuschnigg provided the opportunity Hitler had been seeking. Schuschnigg had been experiencing problems with Austrian Nazis and a plot to stage a coup in Vienna. Hitler therefore demanded that Austria complied with German demands and declare an amnesty for political prisoners, mainly Austrian Nazis. To further increase pressure on the Austrian Government, he ordered military manoeuvres near the Austrian frontier.

However, Schushnigg was undeterred by the Führer's growing resentment towards him and tried frantically to retrieve the worsening situation. To this end, on 12 March 1938 he announced a plebiscite on the question of the independence of Austria . Since the voting was restricted to those over 24 years old (many Nazi supporters were young men), and all Nazi members were denied the vote, Hitler felt compelled to draw up military plans to commit Germany to an unwanted invasion of Austria.

Slowly, hour by hour, Hitler began raising the stakes against the Austrian Government and the Austrian president, Wilhelm Miklas, with the threat of a military invasion. During the evening of 11 March, Schuschnigg, who was soon to be replaced as chancellor by Artur von Seyss-Inquart, was forced to reassure the Nazi leadership on radio that the Austrian Army would in no way oppose a German invasion. Hitler was relieved. Not only had he been worried at the prospect of spilling the blood of fellow Germans, he was also concerned at the prospect of foreign intervention.

ABOVE: A Horch medium cross-country car displaying the divisional emblem on its right mudguard as well as the tactical sign of an infantry division on its left mudguard. The vehicle has been fitted with a metal frame on the left mudguard for a command flag. The driver, with the rank of *Gefreiter*, or lance corporal, slowly negotiates a small, wooden bridge with the aid of his comrades as he passes over the Austrian border. All three soldiers are wearing the German Army regulation-issue uniform 'tunic', or *Waffenrock*. The soldier standing behind the Horch car is wearing a rifle ammunition pouch.

LEFT: Soldiers dismantle a wooden frontier command gate dividing Austria and Germany. The men also appear to be clearing the road of rocks and other obstructions and filling in holes to allow vehicles to pass through. Crossing the Austrian frontier was well publicized; propaganda showed troops 'gloriously' re-uniting with their Austrian 'brothers'. However, the date of this photograph was prior to the official border crossing, made on 13 March 1938. Although the German Army did not officially cross into Austria until 13 March, preparations were made in a number of places with the complete cooperation of Austrian border police.

At 08.00 hours on 13 March, Hitler's troops began streaming into Austria, and at some points frontier barriers were even dismantled by Austrian civilians themselves. This was more like a glorious parade than a military invasion. As armour, horse-drawn transport and infantry poured into Austria, ecstatic women and children shouted and screamed 'Sieg Heil!' and bombarded them with flowers. Panzers were decorated with greenery and flags from both nations. The atmosphere in Austria was engulfed with an excitement beyond belief. Even Hitler himself cried with joy. *Anschluss* (political union) with Austria had finally begun.

SUDETENLAND

While Hitler triumphantly drove into Austria following its bloodless conquest, he remarked to his companion, General Franz Halder, 'this will be very inconvenient to the Czechs'. This was an understatement. The *Anschluss* had seriously disrupted the political and military balance in Czechoslovakia. However, unlike Austria, Czechoslovakia had a powerful army. Even before 1933, Hitler had regarded the country as particularly dangerous, especially with its political ties with Britain and France. But almost immediately following the annexation of Austria, he began putting forward plans to claim the Sudetenland, an area of Czechoslovakia inhabited mainly by German-speaking Czechs. Hitler had said he would no longer tolerate the Sudeten German people being oppressed by the Czech Government. On 20 May 1938, he presented to his generals an interim draft for an attack on Czechoslovakia, codenamed Operation 'Green'. In response to German troop movements, the Czech Government ordered a partial mobilization, and Britain and France warned Germany of the consequences if she took any military action. It was here, against Czechoslovakia, that Hitler intended to first use his lightning war, or *Blitzkrieg*, tactics. The impact of fast-moving armour and air superiority was crucial to the *Blitzkrieg* concept. By employing this new type of warfare, Hitler was sure that it would only be a matter of days before Czechoslovakia was defeated and under German control.

Both Britain and France became increasingly embroiled in the argument. The governments of both countries urged the Czechs to make concessions to the Sudeten Germans. Britain was quite prepared for Germany to annex the Sudetenland, as long as she did it by negotiation. There were further threats from Hitler, but they were not needed. At the Munich Conference, Hitler managed to secure from Britain's Prime Minister, Neville Chamberlain and the French Premier, Edouard Daladier, the ceding of the Sudetenland to Germany. It was all done without consultation with the Czechs.

When the *Wehrmacht* finally rolled into the Sudetenland on 1 October 1938, they were again received with open arms. Thousands of Sudeten Germans filled the roads, littering villages and towns with flowers and greeting soldiers with glasses of schnapps. These were joyous moments for the German soldiers, for they had been welcomed as blood brothers or liberators. However, their next move in Europe would not be so welcomed.

ABOVE: In a number of places along the Austrian border, moving heavy equipment by horse-drawn transport and armoured vehicles was hindered by bad road surfaces. Some bridges were regarded as impassable by heavy armour and could only be re-strengthened by wooden scaffolding. Here officers watch *RAD* and *Wehrmacht* troops cut down pine trees that littered the Austrian and German border. They are preparing the logs for use on some of the more impassable roads and bridges in the area. Although none of the soldiers are heavily armed, one, who appears to be a motorcyclist, is armed with an M1924 stick-grenade that has been pushed through his rifle ammunition pouch. The stick-grenade was primed by pulling on a cord in the base of the handle before throwing it. The soldier then had just less than five seconds to throw the grenade (overarm) before it detonated. However the *Anschluss* with Austria was to pass off peacefully.

OCCUPATION OF CZECHOSLOVAKIA

Despite Hitler's bloodless conquest of the Sudetenland, he was dissatisfied with the Munich Agreement, seeing it as an attempt by the West to stem Germany's freedom of manoeuvre and to prevent his ambitions in the East. He was determined that the 'pathetic' piece of paper he had signed would not stop him guaranteeing Czechoslovakia's boundaries, and saw the continued existence of an independent Czechoslovakia as intolerable.

Just three weeks after the *Wehrmacht*'s triumphant march into the Sudetenland he began taking steps to eliminate Czechoslovakia entirely. Whereas previously he had used the Sudeten Germans against the Czechs, he was now going to use the Slovaks in a similar role. For five months, Hitler tried to encourage the Slovaks to claim complete independence. When the Czechs responded to resentment over the Slovaks' moves for separatism, and dismissed the Slovak Government on 9 March 1939, Hitler seized the opportunity and made his move. Five days later, the Czech Government desperately attempted to avert a German invasion. Hitler was unmoved, and threatened the Czech President, Emil Hácha, with the bombing of Prague if his troops did not lay down their arms. After suffering a heart attack, Hácha agreed to sign a communiqué which placed the fate of Czechoslovakia in Hitler's hands.

On 15 March 1939, Hitler's armies occupied Bohemia and Moravia and, on 23 March, they annexed Memel, a Lithuanian city inhabited by ethnic Germans. Within two weeks following his victorious entry into Memel, on 3 April 1939, Hitler had drawn up a most secret directive to the armed forces, inaugurating Operation 'White', the codename for the invasion of Poland.

ABOVE: Dawn on 13 March 1938; two *Wehrmacht* soldiers and their commanding officer march towards the Austrian border to ceremonially open the town's barrier in front of a jubilant crowd of Austrians. Only 24 hours earlier, Hitler had approved plans to invade Austria if the Austrian Government would not agree to his terms. All over the country, local Nazis were already seizing town halls and government offices and waiting eagerly for word that the frontier had been crossed and *Anschluss* with Austria had been effectively secured.

BELOW: Jubilation as German troops cross into Austria. Hundreds of elated children lining the road into a village cheer and wave and give the Nazi salute as evidence of their support for the *Anschluss*. Many of the children were dressed in either their 'Sunday best' or the national costume, and had gathered flowers together to line the routes of the endless German troop convoys. This was no propaganda photograph, but a shot taken by a passing soldier as he entered the first village of many during his long journey towards Vienna.

ABOVE: Soldiers are overwhelmed by the locals of this village and cannot resist to stop and toast the *Anschluss* with a glass of wine. The soldiers have been decorated by the women with the symbol of Austria, the edelweiss. Two soldiers appear to be wearing the old-style waterproof motorcycle coat, a popular, practical item which was worn with army canvas-and-leather issue gloves or cloth mittens, with overshoes and leggings, or with army boots. Note the gas-mask canisters: these were worn for comfort in vehicles or on motorcycles, normally slung around the neck instead of across the back.

BELOW: Austrian children get the chance to observe and feel a real German weapon of war: a 3.7cm (1.45in) PaK 35/36 antitank gun, the standard antitank gun of the German Army. It weighed only 432kg (952.5lb) and had a sloping splinted shield. The barrel was 42 calibres in length and fired a solid-shot round at a muzzle velocity of 762m/s (2500ft/s) to a maximum range of 4025m (4400yd). The gun was easily capable of penetrating 48m (1.9in) of armour at the vertical or 36mm (1.4in) of 30° sloped armour. In Poland the gun proved its worth against the enemy armour which had limited protection for its crews.

BELOW: Troops enjoy glass of white wine along with their officers as they celebrate the *Anschluss* on 13 March 1938. Note the soldier with the rank of *Hauptfeldwebel* (quartermaster) on the right, and his commanding officer on the left, both wearing leather map-pouches. Within days of the triumphant entry into Austria, 99.08 per cent of Nazi Germany voted their approval of Hitler's actions. In Austria itself, the figure was higher still: 99.75 per cent were in favour. Troops would gather around and listen to their Führer express his gratitude for the *Anschluss* and say 'this was the proudest hour of my life'.

LEFT: On the road to Vienna following Hitler's triumphant entry on 14 March 1938, a group of soldiers consider how they are going to extricate this *leichte Panzerspähwagenleichte* SdKfz 221 that has become stuck in a roadside ditch. This four-wheeled 3.75 tonne (4.1 ton) vehicle was armed with a 2cm (0.79in) KwK 30 cannon and co-axial 7.92mm (0.31in) MG 34 machine gun mounted in an open-topped rotating turret. It was powered by a 56kW (75hp) Auto Union Horch eight-cylinder petrol engine and had a maximum road speed of 80km/h (50mph) with an operational road range of 280km (174 miles). Across country, however, it could only manage 32km/h (20mph) with an operational range of just 200km (124.5 miles).

ABOVE: Three very young Austrian children are seated inside a Horch cross-country car. The boy on the left is wearing a M1938 *Feldmütz*, whilst the boy on the right is wearing an M1935 steel helmet. Behind them is a rolled up *Zeltbahn*, which has been strapped to the rear of the vehicle. The *Zeltbahn* – or waterproof shelter triangle – was made of drill and was issued universally throughout the German Army. When not in use, it was folded or rolled and worn strapped onto the wearer's field equipment. Two could be joined together to form a shelter. It was an essential item in bad weather.

ABOVE: Finally putting aside any worries of a European war, at dawn on 1 October 1938, German troops crossed the border between Germany and the German-speaking nation of the Sudetenland. Here in an old 1920s truck a group of German journalists from the Ministry of Propaganda have their photograph taken as they pass beneath the opening border barrier into the Sudetenland. In contrast, journalists were not allowed to write about the falling public morale in Germany. Hitler was still confident that the Munich Agreement would settle the score with Czechoslovakia forever.

ABOVE: On the Sudetenland/German border, locals come to greet German troops who are about to raise the frontier barrier and march through. A woman can be seen warmly shaking hands with an officer who has just received a bunch of flowers. Although a number of Sudetenland photographs were staged for propaganda purposes, this shot from a soldier's personal camera reveals the true elation of this small village community. Flags and other Nazi pennants can be seen fluttering from the windows of a hotel, revealing the Sudeten Germans' desire for the apparent benefits of annexation by the German Reich.

ABOVE: October 1938; inquisitive Sudeten children play around an eight-wheeled SdKfz 263. This vehicle was issued to the *Nachricten Abteilung* of motorized infantry and panzer divisions as well as Corps and Army headquarters. The SdKfz 263 radio vehicle was equipped with a long-range radio set. Canvas covers protect the crew compartment and telescoping mast antenna. When these vehicles attacked Poland a year later in September 1939, many were seen with special metal boxes attached to the side, containing hand grenades.

RIGHT: A column of Horch cross-country cars, motorcyclists with sidecar combination, SdKfz 231 heavy eight-wheeled armoured cars and a multitude of other vehicles cross onto the Sudetenland. As for the thronging crowds lining the road, these soldiers had not seen jubilation like this since the *Anschluss* with Austria. Many soldiers felt a sense of duty and were proud of taking part in another bloodless conquest where German-speaking people were at last re-united with the Reich. In just five years after coming to power, Hitler had raised Germany from one of the lowest points of her history to the position of being a leading power in Europe.

RIGHT: A line of motorcyclists with sidecar combination receive a tumultuous welcome from the inhabitants of a Sudeten town on 5 October 1938. Flower chains and bouquets of flowers are thrown to the passing column, while some people show their support with shouts of *'Sieg Heil'* and Nazi salutes. The second motorcycle from the front has been equipped with a heavy bar mount to mount the MG 34 machine gun on the sidecar so that it could be fired while the motorcycle was in motion.

BELOW: Lines of German soldiers watch a number of armoured vehicles pass through a Sudeten village on 5 October 1938. An SdKfz 263 is the last of the armoured vehicles to pass by. M98a rifles can be seen stacked together with MG 34 machine guns. This little procession was more than likely a display of military might, as a number of Sudeten border police and civilians can be seen engaged in watching the spectacle. The number and intensity of military parades such as these were to heighten in the early years of victory for Germany during her *Blitzkrieg* campaign. Warsaw, Paris and then Tripoli were three main events where the Germans were to display their military strength and hardware to maximum propaganda effect.

ABOVE: A motorcycle combination has passed through another jubilant Sudeten town. Scenes such as this were common throughout the German-speaking part of Czechoslovakia. But even as these German forces marched victoriously through the streets, hailed as liberators, Hitler, along with his top military advisors, was already engaged in drawing up the necessary plans for executing his next move: the forthcoming attack against Bohemia and Moravia.

RIGHT: October 1938: Sudeten people rejoice by painting pro-Nazi slogans prior to a German military invasion. Horch cross-country cars pass through an unguarded border point. In some places, Sudeten border police climbed on board armoured vehicles to join in celebration. The occupation of the Sudetenland was completed between 1 and 10 October 1938. Almost all of Czechoslovakia's fortifications had been captured without a shot being fired.

BELOW: A banner reads 'We thank you our Führer' as more German vehicles pour into the Sudetenland. Throughout Germany, newspapers published complete pictorial spreads of the bloodless conquest. Hitler had used the press for both the annexation of Austria and the Sudetenland as an effective propaganda weapon. To Hitler, 1938 was not the end of what he called 'an historical epoch', but was 'only the beginning of a great historic epoch of our nation'. For him, Czechoslovakia, with a modern army and significant military resources, was a troublesome threat to Germany's south-eastern flank.

LEFT: Soldiers read new posters that have been pasted across many of the towns and villages of the Sudetenland. The left-hand headline reads: 'SA Marching', followed by an appeal to Sudeten Germans to take positive action in the cause for self-determination. The right-hand poster calls for volunteers to join the *Wehrmacht*. Between 1 and 10 October 1938, the *Wehrmacht* established itself along the entire new Czecho-slovak frontier, overlooking nervous Czech forces in their makeshift defences. The threat of an invasion was a constant fear that gripped the entire nation of Czecho-slovakia for five long months.

ABOVE: An SdKfz 263 passes through a Sudeten village, with some of the locals giving the Nazi salute as the vehicle moves past them. The vehicle's commander is wearing the panzer *Schutzmütze* or panzer beret, and the special black panzer uniform worn by the new panzer arm of the German Army. This special style of uniform was designed, manufactured and issued to be worn by all the men all ranks who served in armoured fighting vehicles.

ABOVE: A Czech commanding officer formally hands over his army headquarters to a German officer on 5 September 1938. The white flag the Czech soldier is holding is a formal declaration of the surrender. In a number of areas in the Sudetenland, the Czech Army formally handed over provinces, or towns and villages. But in other parts, especially along the frontier with Czechoslovakia, officers sometimes ordered their men to leave quietly and avoid humiliation.

BELOW: A German officer standing to attention in his Horch cross-country car salutes a Sudeten police chief. With the deployment of military forces in the Sudetenland, police officials were an important asset for restoring stability among German-speaking Sudetens and Czechs. Many of them could not only speak fluent Czech, but they also made very good informants, especially against those elements they regarded as Czech sympathizers or anti-Nazis.

ABOVE: With the aid of scissor binoculars, a German infantryman points out Germany, the great Fatherland, in the distance to a young Sudeten child. As were the children in Austria, Sudeten children were ruthlessly indoctrinated into the ideals of a new, greater German Reich. The annexation of both countries would bring a huge wave of new members into the *Hitlerjugend* (Hitler Youth) which, by the end of 1938, had reached a total membership of 8,700,000 young people.

RIGHT: Sudeten children pose in front of the camera, giving the Nazi salute, at an unguarded border-control point at Sebastiansberg. One of the boys shown here is dressed in a full *Hitlerjugend* uniform. Soon most of his friends were compelled to join the *Hitlerjugend* as an aggressive recruiting programme swept the Sudetenland. Even before the annexation of Austria and the Sudetenland, the German 'Propaganda Office' of the *Reichsjugendführung* – which was responsible for *Hitlerjugend* periodicals – founded a book club with the specific objective of spreading the word of National Socialism to thousands of Austrian and Czech children.

LEFT: A group of Sudeten girls give a passing German vehicle their support and raise their right arm in salute of their beloved 'Führer'. These girls were soon absorbed into the *Deutscher Mädel* for domestication. According to Nazi ideology, girls were expected to grow up to be good housewives with large families. They were told to produce pure children for the Fatherland and to be strong and obedient mothers. The motto for girls in the *Deutscher Mädel* was, 'Be faithful, be pure, be German!' During 1938, the German 'Propaganda Office' of the *Reichsjugendführung* offered all Sudeten children, boys and girls, the chance to obtain books – full of National Socialist propaganda – at low cost. The Propaganda Office especially targeted its literature at the young people of other German-speaking countries in Europe.

BELOW: Soldiers pose with a group of local Sudeten children on 6 October 1938, sitting in a Horch medium cross-country car. The children are wearing M1935 helmets and two of the girls an M1938 *Feldmütze*. A number of propaganda photographs published in the Reich during this period show exhilarated children with German troops. This private photograph was taken at the request of the children's parents, who saw the annexation as a proud moment in their country's history.

ABOVE: Although this photograph can quickly be misinterpreted as showing that fighting has begun with Czech forces, the rising black smoke is actually a border control point being blown up. This photograph was more than likely to have been taken by a dispatch rider as his motorcycle combination stands in full view. Note the tactical markings painted on the front of the sidecar. The number '3' indicates that it is from the 3rd Company of the 20th Motorized Division.

BELOW: In the town of Görkau, Czech police and troops are being frisked for hidden weapons as tension along the border with Czechoslovakia heightens. The German soldiers are all wearing the standard kit worn by troops of this period. Of particular interest is the army dispatch rider (centre left) who wears goggles normally issued to Luftwaffe flight crews. He is carrying an ammunition case, which suggests that the soldiers expected some of kind of localized resistance.

BELOW: A parade of the drum and fife section, including regimental bandsmen and trumpeters, play to the jubilation of liberated Sudetens. Note the musicians' 'swallows' nests, or *Schwalbennester*, which were musicians' wings. These were a traditional item dress decoration which showed the wearer's branch of service, as well as indicating that he was a military musician. This particular event, held in the town of Bodenbach, took place on 3 October 1938.

ABOVE: Inside a Mercedes-Benz 770G4 W31, *Bürgermeister* Kreissl is sitting next to General Walther von Brauchitsch. To the overwhelming sounds of a military band and a chorus of singing children, they enter the ancient market place of Bodenbach on 3 October 1938. Only the day before

Brauchitsch, Erhard Milch, Fritz Todt and Hitler flew from Berlin for a flying tour of the newly-regained Sudeten lands. A month earlier – even as late as 28 September – Brauchitsch had tried to rally the German generals to oppose Hitler's plans for an invasion of Czechoslovakia.

RIGHT: Soldiers and Sudeten civilians line the market place in Bodenbach town centre on 3 October 1938 to pay homage to General Brauchitsch and *Bürgermeister* Kreissl. Hundreds of soldiers and civilians salute. Shouts of *'Sieg Heil!'* from the tumultuous crowd drown out the military band. The day before, Hitler visited the newly-occupied land. 'Its scale was brought home to me', he said, 'only at the moment I stood for the first time in the midst of the Czech fortress line: ... I realized what it means to have captured a front line of almost two thousand kilometres of fortifications without having fired a single shot in anger.'

ABOVE: From a balcony overlooking Bodenbach market square, Brauchitsch speaks to some of the troops from the 20th Motorized Division and the civilians of the town. The photograph's original caption states that Brauchitsch is telling his troops that they have awarded the Sudetens a place in history and given them honour and pride. The historic visit to Bodenbach was not to go unnoticed by the Ministry of Propaganda. Keen not to miss an photo opportunity, two party camera men can be seen, one filming from a window and the other clinging to the side of the balcony to get a better shot.

BELOW: During the same procession, motorcycle combinations, armoured personnel carriers towing PaK 35/36 antitank guns and a variety of other vehicles pour through the town. The Pak 35/36 gun was the most popular gun in the German Army in 1938. By September 1939, the German army fielded some 11,200 PaK 35/36 guns. They were to be so effective in the war against the Poles that even the *SS-Verfügungs* Division, later to become known as the *Waffen-SS*, raised two additional motorized antitank battalions, using a number of PaK 35/36 guns for the war against the West in 1940.

ABOVE: Brauchitsch completes another stirring speech to the Sudeten people. While he and the commander of the 20th Motorized Division take the salute, party faithful and Sudeten Nazis scream *'Sieg Heil!'* and begin emotionally to sing, *'Deutschland über alles'*. It was important to the Nazis to plant seeds of National Socialism in all German-speaking countries that fell under the yoke of Nazi rule. Speeches like this one, transmitted across the rest of the Reich, also helped bring unity and settle thoughts of uneasiness, especially to some of the citizens of Germany who feared another European war.

ABOVE: Troops from the 20th Motorized Division march past Sudeten Nazis during a parade. The standard bearer can just be seen wearing the German Army regimental standard bearer gorget, of National Socialist design. The bosses, oakleaves and design are of a bronzed-colour finish. There were six known varieties of gorgets worn by army personnel during the period between 1933 and the end of the war in 1945.

BELOW: Sudeten locals watch more armoured vehicles pour across the border. Even before the Germans entered the Sudetenland, men, women and children were seen destroying border points and painting pro-Nazi slogans across the entrance. This photograph is evidence of the frenzied attacks made on the border control points. The barrier has been totally demolished: dynamite may well have been used.

BELOW: This photograph has been taken just inside the entrance of a former Czech Army barracks, now occupied by units of the 20th Motorized Division. The soldier on the left is wearing an army marksmanship lanyard which indicates to an observer that he has been awarded for his skill with a variety of weapons. He is more than likely to be on guard duty as the lanyard was permitted to be worn with the guard uniform. Behind him is an SdKfz 221 light armoured car.

CHAPTER TWO

Blitzkrieg Unleashed

The Attack on Poland

As long as the city of Danzig, which was populated almost exclusively by German-speaking people, and the 'Polish Corridor' existed as they were, there would be no lasting peace between Poland and Germany. Being separated from East Prussia by a corridor that gave Poland access to the sea bitterly angered Hitler. By August 1939, the quarrel over the city of Danzig and the 'Polish Corridor' brought both nations to the brink of war. For the first time Hitler was confronted by a country that was resolute and determined to defend itself to the hilt if it were attacked.

Just days before the invasion of Poland was unleashed, Hitler told his Eastern Front commanders that the war with Poland would be a different type of warfare than had been seen in Europe before, not like the dehumanizing years of trench warfare in the 1914–18 war, but a new concept, *Blitzkrieg*: swift, all-out attack of such force and ferocity that victory would be secured quickly and decisively. Thus, as the last steps towards war were inaugurated, Hitler put the finishing touches to what he called his war of 'liberation'. The faked 'Polish' attacks on German border positions at Pitschen and Gleiwitz were concocted by Hitler to 'prove' to the outside world that it was Poland, not the mighty Germany, who had begun hostilities first.

INVASION OF POLAND

During the early hours of 1 September 1939, German aircraft began leaving their home bases for Poland. From all their assigned airfields, the *Luftwaffe* attacked Polish targets. Airfields, aviation production centres, troop

LEFT: Just before 04.40 hours on 1 September 1939, along huge stretches of the German and Polish border, the German Third, Fourth, Eighth, Tenth, and Fourteenth armies began shelling Polish positions. For nearly an hour, explosions burst out all along the frontier.

FAR LEFT: A column of troops and horse-drawn transport pass a field kitchen on a very congested road in central Poland. During the campaign miles of slow-moving traffic, as well as thousands of refugees, hindered the panzers' movement.

concentrations, ammunition dumps, railways, bridges, and open cities were bombed. Within minutes of the first attacks, German warplanes were giving the unprepared Poles the first taste of sudden death and destruction from the skies ever to have been experienced on any great scale on Earth.

On the ground, 52 divisions and an armoured force of formidable tanks drove swiftly across the Polish heartlands to achieve Germany's first tactical gains. Following in the rear, German soldiers were moved forward into action, their path forced open principally by tanks that had rammed and overrun obstacles. The Poles were overwhelmed by the German onslaught. The sudden surprise attack; the bombers and fighters soaring overhead, reconnoitring, attacking, spreading fire and fear; the Stukas howling as they dived; the tanks, whole divisions of them breaking through along even the most rutted Polish roads; the amazing speed of the infantry, of the whole huge army of a million and a half men on a mixture of horses, wheels, and tracks, was directed and coordinated through a complicated maze of intricate radio, telephone and telegraph networks.

LEFT: German troops from Blaskowitz's 30th Infantry Division of Eighth Army move through one of the first of many badly bombed Polish towns. Judging by the extent of the damage, it was probably caused by heavy *Luftwaffe* attacks. Throughout the first few days especially, the *Luftwaffe* mercilessly attacked Polish airfields, aviation production centres, troop concentrations, ammunition dumps, railways, and bridges. Towns and cities were also bombed.

TWO ARMY GROUPS

To carry out this monumental task against Poland, there were two Army Groups: Army Group North, consisting of the Fourth and Third armies, under the command of General Fedor von Bock, and Army Group South, consisting of the Eighth, Tenth, and Fourteenth armies, under the command of General Gerd von Rundstedt. From the north to the south, all five German armies crashed over the frontier.

Spearheading one of the first attacks into Poland from the north was General Gunther Hans von Kluge's Fourth Army. Kluge controlled five infantry divisions, plus two motorized divisions and the 3rd Panzer Division under General Heinz Guderian. Further east, separated by the Polish corridor in East Prussia, General George von Küchler's Third Army made a number of thrusting all-out attacks south of the Polish Corridor in the direction of Warsaw against the Polish Narew Group and Modlin Army.

ABOVE: On the edge of a Polish forest an MG 34 machine-gun crew scour a field while their comrades play chess. The MG 34 is on a tripod mounting for sustained fire. The first machine gun to be designed as both a light and heavy machine gun, it could also be used with a bipod. The MG 34 could either fire a 'saddle' magazine or use 250-round belts with a rate of fire of 800–900 rounds per minute. The machine gun weighed 11.5kg (25.4lb) and had a muzzle velocity of 762m/s (2500ft/s). Because this gun could deliver a formidable volume of fire, the Poles quickly came to treat the German weapon with respect.

LEFT: More troops belonging to the 30th Infantry Division pass through yet another destroyed Polish town. Although the German Army was ultimately the most modern, superior, well-equipped army anywhere in the world, much of its logistics still relied heavily on horses. In the wake of the great armoured strike across Poland, horse-drawn transport was at times inevitably left far behind, and this lack of support would, in some places, cause the front to become overstretched, a problem which was to repeat itself during the invasion of the Soviet Union in 1941, with dire consequences.

Under his command advanced seven infantry divisions, an *ad hoc* SS panzer division, and four brigade-sized commands, all divided into three corps. To the south, German forces were inflicting almost equal misery upon the enemy.

With lightning speed, German ground forces, together with aerial support, strove to achieve their objectives. The commander of Eighth Army, General Johannes von Blaskowitz, drove his four infantry divisions in the direction of Lodz against the Lodz Army. On Eighth Army's southern flank, General Walter von Reichenau's Tenth Army launched a series of infantry attacks together with two armoured divisions consisting of General Reinhardt's 4th Panzer Division and General Schmidt's 1st Panzer Division. The 4th Panzer Division was the strongest division in the entire German Army and was given the most difficult task of driving on Warsaw. On Tenth Army's southern flank, General List's Fourteenth Army, comprising of some seven infantry and two armoured divisions, made staggering advances against the Krakow and Carpathian armies. In just several hours, List's force had catapulted across the frontier and burst into the Polish heartlands. It was far ahead of schedule.

The entire thrust of the German Army was quick and swift. The fruits of the great dash east were intoxicating for the men who rode the tanks and trucks in an almost unopposed advance across country against a disorganized jumble of Polish units. Over the next few days, both the German Northern and Southern groups continued to make furious thrusts on all fronts. Combined with air and powerful armoured strikes, in just five days of unbroken combat, Kluge's Fourth Army had cut the Polish Corridor,

established a 'bridge' between Pomerania and East Prussia, and encircled thousands of enemy soldiers from the Poznan and Pomorze Army. South of the country, operations were moving as rapidly as in the north. The bulk of Blaskowitz's Eighth Army maintained a steady drive on Lodz, but units found themselves confounded by the appalling traffic jams caused by refugees and by Polish Army vehicles entangled on the roads strafed by air attack. Most vehicles, particularly panzers, struck off across country to escape the chaos and continue the lightning advance forward.

Only on the roads did the traffic slow, the dust billowing, choking men and horses, and stifling motors. All along Reichenau's front, unceasing attacks embraced the dwindling enemy lines. For striking power, the mighty Tenth relied on its tremendous superiority in tanks and artillery. Reinhardt's 4th Panzer Division's armoured strike was now threatening the Polish capital. By the evening of 8 September, advanced elements of 4th Panzer had arrived on the outskirts of Warsaw and attempted to storm it. However, the city was well defended; the attack failed, with the loss of 57 armoured vehicles.

FIGHTING ON THE RIVERS

On 9 September, German forces began arriving on the banks of the River Vistula. Such was their rapid advance that the Poles had not even had time to build a defensive barrier along the river, let alone a network of field fortifications, which had been the intended plan. Before the Vistula, the Germans committed their main forces to wholly unspectacular clearing operations, preparing the front between the rivers Vistula and Bug.

RIGHT: A Junkers Ju52/3m transport aircraft shot down by Polish antiaircraft fire. The Ju52, known as the 'Iron Annie', remained the standard *Luftwaffe* utility vehicle until the end of the war. Two air fleets were used against Poland in 1939, *Luftflotte* I and *Luftflotte* IV, while *Luftflotte* II and *Luftflotte* III were to be released whilst operations against Poland were continuing. Both *Luftflotte* I and *Luftflotte* IV had a total of 1581 fighting aircraft between them: 897 bomb-carrying planes (648 He111, Do17 and Ju86 medium bombers, 219 Ju87 dive-bombers, 30 Hs123 strike aircraft), 210 Bf109 and Bf110 fighters, 474 reconnaissance, transport and other types.

On the Bzura River, remnants of the Poznan and Pomorze armies, now thrown together in one Army commanded by General Kutrzeba, struck General Ulex's X Corps of the Eighth Army. What followed was the largest battle during the Polish campaign. By 10 September, the sheer scale of the battle unfolded, with unconfirmed reports of some 400,000 men embroiled into the fighting, which included parts of the Tenth Army being drawn off from attacks on Warsaw.

Simultaneously, while these battles raged along the Bzura and Vistula, both the Fourth and Third Armies made a series of combined attacks across the Narew, reaching parts of the Bug that were heavily fortified. In the south, List's Army was arriving on the bank of the San and was making combined efforts to destroy all remaining pockets of resistance in the area. By 10 September, the Polish Army had been vanquished. Most of its 30 divisions had been either destroyed or caught in a vast pincer movement that closed around Warsaw. There remained for the Germans the 'Second Phase': crushing the dazed and disorganized Polish units, and destroying them, before completing a second, much deeper, envelopment aimed at the River Bug, 201km (125 miles) east of Warsaw.

DISINTEGRATION

On 12 September 1939, the dispirited and confused Commander-in-Chief of the Polish Army, Marshal Rydz-Smigly, ordered the withdrawal of the entire Polish Army, which had now been divided into the Polish Northern, Central and Southern Groups. These exhausted soldiers were in retreat to the south-eastern parts of the country, and attempted to hold positions until the expected launching of a French offensive. Their retreat had not degenerated into panic, despite the pulverizing effects of the enemies' *Blitzkrieg* tactics. Obstinate defence of every foot of ground became the aim of the Polish leadership. Villages and towns in the objective area were strongly held by a mixture of Polish troops and partisans. But despite this frantic defensive measure, the German onslaught, using fully mechanized panzer divisions supported by the most powerful air force in the world, brought the Poles to their knees.

To make matters worse, on 17 September the Russian Army attacked Poland along its whole frontier from Latvia in the north down to Romania in the south. Germany's new-found ally had been preparing the invasion for weeks. In a secret addendum to their non-aggression pact, drawn up in August 1939, Stalin and Hitler had both agreed to carve up Poland between themselves. For the Polish armies, the situation was now even grimmer. For them, the final blow had been delivered.

By 18 September, besieged by an ever-increasing flow of infantry, tanks and the aerial might of the *Luftwaffe*, the Polish Army disintegrated. German soldiers were completely stunned by the weight and speed of the blow that they had inflicted. The battle of the Bzura alone had resulted in the total destruction of nearly a quarter of the Polish Army. The German victory over Poland had taken no more than 18 days to achieve. What remained were isolated pockets of resistance in a number of towns and

BELOW: A 15cm (5.9in) sFH 18 heavy field howitzer being hitched to an 8(t) halftrack prime mover. When moved by motor vehicle, the howitzer was not broken down, which allowed a far quicker transport of the gun to various sectors of the front than using the slow process of horse-drawn transport.

The gun tractor also had sufficient seating for the entire gun crew. When moved by horse, the howitzer had to be divided into two parts with separate wagons for the barrel and gun carriage. It took the crews much longer to achieve fire readiness, and it also gave them a physically heavy workload.

LEFT: A sFH18 heavy field howitzer crew about to open fire against enemy positions of the Lodz Army. In this picture it can clearly be seen that the howitzer has not been dug in and protected against counterbattery fire, which probably indicates there is little resistance present in the immediate area from the Polish Army. The crew member pictured sitting down at the rear of the gun is more than likely priming the shells ready for battle. With a full, well-trained crew, steady fire from this weapon could be kept up for long periods.

cities. On 21 September, the siege of the city of Lwow ended after 120,000 troops were forced to surrender. Six days later following the bombardment by 400 bombers and dive-bombers and group-attack aircraft – supported by 30 tri-motor transport planes – the defiant city of Warsaw finally surrendered. In the aftermath, a total of 140,000 soldiers were taken into captivity. Following the fall of Warsaw, numerous other engagements, some of them quite heavy, continued to rage until the last Polish units capitulated and laid down their arms on 6 October.

The Polish Army was the first army in Europe to come up against the full fury of the German tactics of *Blitzkrieg*. The Germans had won their battle against Poland by implementing these tactics in a series of overwhelming, rapid penetrations. These penetrations were followed by the encirclement of an enemy that, in contrast to its German counterparts, was bound by static and inflexible defensive tactics. With Poland's defeat, Hitler had secured the key to the East; it would now be the turn of the West to face the might of *Blitzkrieg*.

ABOVE: Soldiers with their commanding officer huddle around a radio and listen to the latest news announced by the German Progaganda Ministry. Regular broadcasts to the front line were the soldiers' main link to the outside world, and news stories were heavily vetted before being transmitted. For example, the majority of German soldiers that fought in Poland were not informed of the declaration of war on Germany by Britain and France on 3 September 1939, as their leaders feared it could lower the men's morale and fighting spirit. In fact, the *Wehrmacht*'s success in Poland meant its morale was sky high.

LEFT: Polish prisoners from the Lodz Army captured on 3 September 1939. By this stage of the war, it was quite evident that Polish generalship fell victim to the inability of the army to match the performance of its skilful opponents on the battlefield. Polish tactics were shown to be not only unimaginative, but also unable to cope with the rapid speed at which events were unfolding. Faced with the collapse of everything that they held dear, the Polish Army displayed more sacrificial courage than their German opponents. Most of the Polish troops the Germans confronted were undertrained, poorly equipped, and demoralized because of the acute lack of ammunition and supplies. On interrogation, it was revealed that these prisoners had not eaten for two days due to a complete breakdown in supply.

RIGHT: The ambitions of nearly every German soldier in Poland were simple: to survive, finish the job, and go home. It was against logic for him to suppose that he would fall victim to enemy fire, but even so, many did. Here, a German soldier has been buried with full military honours and laid to rest beside a Polish war memorial somewhere in northern Poland.

BELOW: A dispatch rider has halted beside a knocked-out Polish vehicle that has probably fallen victim to a Stuka attack. Because of the very hot weather during the campaign, called 'Führer weather', this rider is not wearing his heavy waterproof motorcycle coat. Worn on his field service belt is his gas-mask canister, M1935 leather dispatch case, and rolled-up *Zeltbahn*.

ABOVE: German soldiers rounding up Jews in a burning town. Although this photograph is taken in the early days of the campaign, it would not be until later that the most sinister activities of the war were employed in Poland. Behind the military arm of the *SS-VT* (later the *Waffen-SS*) and *Wehrmacht*, lurked the SS 'Death Head' groups or *Totenkopfvebande* led by Theodor Eicke. Three regiments were deployed for ethnic cleansing: SS *Oberbayern*, *Brandenburg*, and *Thuringen*. In a matter of days, Eicke's men began eradicating Poles who were regarded as hostile elements within the Reich.

LEFT: The soldiers pictured here have come across an unexploded bomb that has been dropped on Polish territory by a German bomber. The *Luftwaffe* wreaked havoc on Polish towns and cities by dropping thousands of tons of bombs from their numerous aircraft. Engineers who were left to deal with the aftermath did not normally risk their lives by trying to defuse an unexploded bomb. Instead, they would usually set to work by first cordoning off the area and evacuating any soldiers and civilians, before blowing the incendiary device up in a controlled way.

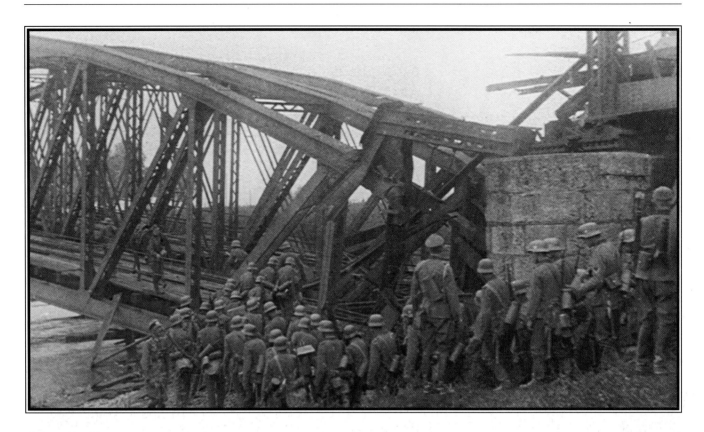

ABOVE: Soldiers, probably a regiment from General Reichenau's Tenth Army, prepare to cross over a partially destroyed bridge on the River Vistula on 9 September 1939. The main rivers in Poland, generally flowing from south to north of the country, formed a barrier against an east-west assault. These were the rivers San, Bzura and Vistula, where the bulk of the fighting took place. The rivers were generally unembankmented, and due to the heavy precipitations of rain and snow, were prone to flooding in spring and autumn. Their Polish defenders therefore sought to exploit these barriers to their best advantage.

ABOVE: The fruits of the great dash east were intoxicating for the men riding the tanks and trucks. An almost unopposed thrust across country, against a disorganized jumble of retreating Polish units, had instilled every German soldier with an eager enthusiasm. Here three soldiers, each armed with M98a rifles, are being moved to the front by horse-drawn transport, passing through yet another smouldering village that has been subjected to heavy bombing by the *Luftwaffe*.

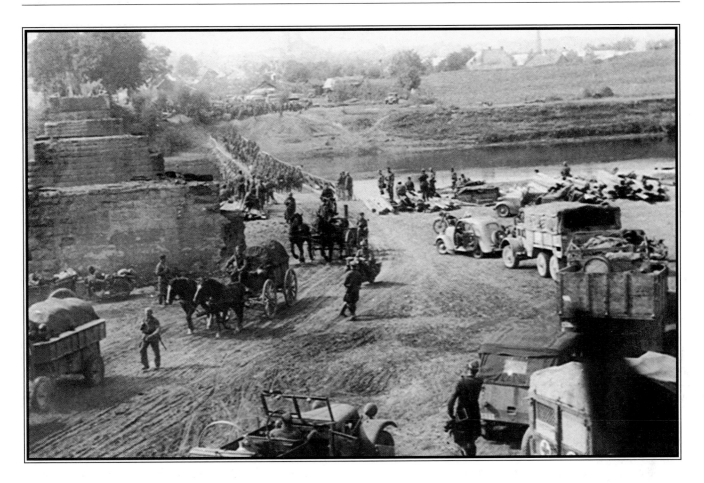

ABOVE: A multitude of various vehicles, some of which are probably in service with the bridge-building units. The vehicles include Horch cross-country cars, Opel-Blitz trucks, a Phänomen Grant ambulance truck, Volkswagen light personnel carrier, and horse-drawn transport, which most probably are carrying ammunition. On the bridge, soldiers can be seen crossing to the other side of the bank. After the German forces had achieved the virtual elimination of the Polish Air Force, its troops could move freely and visibly across rivers without the fear of being attacked from above.

LEFT: A German crossing point has been established on the banks of the River Vistula, on 10 September 1939. Until a strong bridge could be constructed by the army engineers, as much materiel as possible was moved across the river on pontoon rafts by the troops. The necessity of moving such crucial but heavy equipment, especially weighty armour, meant that the troops had little choice but to manhandle it laboriously across the river. Within days, a bridge-building unit would have set about constructing a wooden trestle bridge, which would enable the bulk of these forces from the Tenth Army to cross swiftly and unhindered.

ABOVE: Following in the wake of the armoured spearheads east, infantry became exhausted by the never-ending foot marches that were so common in Poland. By the roadside, a group of soldiers take a much-needed respite. One soldier is using his MG 34 machine gun as a pillow, whilst his comrade is attempting to take a nap by sitting precariously on two ammunition cases. All the soldiers wear the standard issue of kit which consists of M1935 helmet, M98K rifle, gas-mask canister, entrenching tool, bread bag, water bottle, leather map-case, rolled up *Zeltbahn*, and an ammunition box with spares. This ammunition box was a very important asset and would be kept close to a soldier at all times.

ABOVE: A destroyed Polish armoured vehicle near Lodz on 10 September 1939. This vehicle belonged to a Polish cavalry brigade. In total there were 11 cavalry brigades supporting the infantry divisions, which were considered to be the élite of the Polish Army. Each brigade had 3 or 4 cavalry regiments, a reconnaissance squadron of 13 tankettes, and an assortment of armoured cars. These vehicles were antiquated, slow, and not even a match for the German PzKpfw I, the smallest tank in the German Army. Even the light PaK 35/36 antitank gun could easily bring one of these vehicles to a flaming halt.

RIGHT: A German mortar team wait for fire orders in their hastily-dug position on a Polish plain. The team commander keeps watch for any enemy movement with his binoculars. Their relatively exposed position suggests that they are not expecting attack either from the air or from Polish artillery. The mortar was a popular form of heavy support for the infanty: it was mobile and relatively easy to transport. This example is an 8cm (3.2in) sGrW 34, which was used throughout the war. A practised, veteran mortar crew could have several rounds in the air before the first landed, giving their unfortunate targets no time to react or seek shelter.

RIGHT: A German sign has been erected along the Vistula laying down the new boundaries between Germany and Russia. The sign was to indicate to the troops the establishment of the Russian/German demarcation line that had been agreed in addition to the secret non-aggression pact drawn up with Stalin in August 1939. Both Russia and Germany planned to carve up Poland between themselves, and it was first agreed that the Vistula would be the demarcation line with Russia. However, at the end of September 1939, following the Russian invasion, the demarcation line changed. Henceforth the line would be along the Bug down to the San to the Slovakian border.

LEFT: A soldier belonging to Blaskowitz's 30th Infantry Division of Eighth Army has fallen victim to strong enemy fire from undestroyed parts of the Poznan and Pomorze armies in an area south of the town of Kutno. On 11 September 1939, it was General Blaskowitz who was given the order to coordinate the crushing of the 'cauldron' and the destruction of the trapped Polish forces inside. One of the key aims of the Blitzkrieg was to encircle an enemy force and then reduce it with overwhelming firepower – hence the enemy were trapped in a 'cauldron'. This manoeuvre was known as a *Kesselschlacht*. The following day the Poles launched another fierce unremitting attack against the Eighth Army units to the south. Although the Germans managed to effectively halt the advance, it was not done without heavy loss.

LEFT: A group of soldiers from the 30th Infantry Division following the successful halt of strong enemy forces near Kutno. Two of the men, one a motorcyclist, are sitting on a PaK 35/36 antitank gun. This gun had served as an effective weapon during the Polish counteroffensive in the area. Note the dispatch rider dressed in an old-style waterproof motorcycle coat. This protective clothing would have been manufactured out of field grey rubberized cotton twill, with all seams waterproofed. The dispatch rider can be seen wearing his gas-mask canister and M1935 dispatch case. The soldier posing with his hands on his hips is armed with a Luger, probably a 9mm Pistole 38; its black leather holster can be seen hanging from his belt.

LEFT: Another photograph of the same PaK 35/36 antitank gun crew, shown here posing in front of the camera. The picture was taken on 15 September 1939. It appears that this gun has been covered in foliage; this was evidently done in order to conceal it from the prowling eye of the enemy. During the counteroffensive – which this gun crew were involved with – both VI Corps and XVI Panzer Corps had been detached from the Tenth Army in order that they might assist with the attacks on the Polish defences. Although this lessened the pressure on the Warsaw defenders, by 15 September the Polish forces commanded by General Kutrzeba had been finally reduced to nothing more than a small and weakened fighting pocket around the town of Kutno.

ABOVE: Positions west of Warsaw showing soldiers and their commanding officers from an infantry division of Eighth Army who are helping secure the encirclement of Kutrzeba's battered army from the east. By this period, surviving parts of Kutrzeba's force were still continuing to set up improvised defences. However this force was rapidly deteriorating and their efforts could not change the inevitable outcome. Regrouping troops inside the encirclement had become such an impossible task that the majority of Poles simply began to make their way eastwards in an uncoordinated, hasty retreat.

LEFT: A 10.5cm (4.1in) leFH18, the standard light howitzer used by the German Army, pictured here dug in outside a village somewhere near Warsaw. The photo was taken in mid–September 1939. The shells which would be used for this weapon can be clearly seen in the foreground, set in rows in their specially designed wooden crates that were used to transport them safely across some of the worst roads in Poland. Many of the latter were little more than dirt tracks with deep ruts that were covered in dust. Shells were not primed until the gun reached its new fire position. From the lack of empty shell cases, it appears that the gun crew have not yet used the weapon from this location and are still waiting for their fire orders.

RIGHT: An exhausted group of soldiers can be seen lying in a field, trying to snatch some rest, following more or less a continuous unopposed march across Polish land for 10 days. A column of horse-drawn transport can also be seen advancing up the road just ahead of where the soldiers have stopped. As horses were to play a significant role in the task of conquering Poland, this meant that they too were not immune from fatigue and the endless, punishing distances they were forced to cover to keep up with the panzers. Their load was often huge; rather than using motorized transport, the Germans used them to pull artillery, ammunition carts, field kitchens, soldiers, bridge-laying equipment and other important materiel, all of which was needed to sustain the rapid spearhead across Poland.

ABOVE: An interesting photograph which shows the vast scale and absolute reliance on horse-drawn power during the *Blitzkrieg* campaign in Poland. Two horses are pulling a 10.5cm (4.1in) leFH18 light howitzer along the west bank of the River Vistula. Behind the gun, literally hundreds of horses and riders are visible for as far as the eye can see.

ABOVE: Along the Vistula near Deblin, troops examine an abandoned bunker that was supposed to help defend the banks of the river. A variety of equipment, including the bulk of the soldiers' personal kit with M1935 helmet can be seen strapped to the horses' back for ease of carriage. Despite some intense fighting in the area, the soldiers' lack of steel helmet and personal equipment suggests that they are not too close to the front lines. On the Vistula, between Deblin and Annopol, remaining Polish forces from the Radom pocket continued to try and break out east over the river. Those that attempted to escape would charge the solid German lines, but would be virtually annihilated by barrages of artillery and tank strikes. Repeated armoured rushes and infantry assaults slowly ground down the remnants of the enemy. However, despite this heavy mauling, a number of Polish units remained firm and fought back with everything they could muster. To the annoyance of the German High Command, this tied down a number of divisions which were needed elsewhere.

ABOVE: A photograph of a visit to Warsaw by soldiers and officers from the 4th Panzer Division. Although these three burnt-out tramcars do not appear to have been used in the defence of the city as barricades, a number were filled with stones and furniture and used as a crude form of defence. The defence of Warsaw mainly consisted of antitank and flak batteries, including antitank trenches and barricades; some buildings were converted by soldiers into fortified positions. Most barricades were simply furniture and timber that had been erected across the main roads leading into the centre.

RIGHT: Soldiers and their officers from the 4th Panzer Division observe the extent of the destruction of heavy urbanized fighting in the suburbs of Warsaw. Advanced elements of General Reinhardt's 4th Panzer Division were given the task of capturing the Polish capital on 8 September 1939. But by the time Reinhardt's units had arrived at the south-western edge of the city, the inhabitants had prepared for its prolonged defence. The first assault through the Ochota suburbs had immediately been repulsed by strong Polish resistance, with the loss of 57 panzers out of the 120 engaged.

LEFT: Just outside Warsaw an armoured vehicle belonging to a regiment of the 4th Panzer Division passes a group of bewildered Polish civilians. The photograph is remarkable: there is no evidence of combat in this area. However, when the Warsaw garrison continued to resist, the *Luftwaffe* ensured the city would be laid to waste, regardless of civilian casualties. Bad weather initially prevented Göring from unleashing a massive aerial attack on the city, but it was only a temporary respite.

ABOVE: Encamped not far from the Bzura, these soldiers – from an unidentified regiment which belonged to the 30th Infantry Division – rest in a field. Their Mauser rifles are stacked together in this way so that they are quickly accessible if they are urgently required to go into action. M1935 helmets and personal equipment have been taken off in the heat of the Polish summer, and lie next to their rifles. The faces of the two soldiers reflect the new confidence of the *Wehrmacht*.

ABOVE: A horse-drawn wagon, probably containing ammunition, is given a helping hand by a group of soldiers after experiencing difficulty moving through the deep, sandy soil in central Poland. Many of the roads were often sandy tracks, and virtually inaccessible to horse-drawn transport. Had the invasion of Poland been postponed any later than September, the German Army would have experienced great logistical problems due to the autumn rains. Many of the vehicles would have become bogged down in a mire of mud, ice and snow, prolonging the campaign by weeks.

RIGHT: This picture shows a wooden crossing which has been hastily erected next to a blown bridge over a river in order to allow Germans soldiers and armour to cross unhindered. A PzKpfw I Ausf A can be seen advancing along the dusty track next to it. This vehicle was fitted with a fixed superstructure in place of a turret and was armed with a ball-mounted machine gun which could be used for local defence. Two radios were carried on the vehicle, the FuG2 and FuG6, and the tank was manned by a three-man crew. However by 1939 it was effectively obsolete.

LEFT: A column of heavily camouflaged medium Horch cross-country cars are travelling along a road somewhere in the region of central Poland. Foliage has been carefully applied to each vehicle in order to camouflage it, and the cars hug the side of the road in an attempt to blend in with the surrounding terrain. Although the Polish Air Force had all been virtually wiped out during the first two days of the *Blitzkrieg* campaign against them, the Poles still possessed a few aircraft – for example the PZL P-37 *Los* bomber and a small line of numerous other fighters – with which they sporadically attacked German infantry and armoured concentrations.

ABOVE: Two low-flying Ju52 transports fly over a long column of troops and horse-drawn transport near to the Vistula at Deblin on 16 September 1939. The *Luftwaffe* divided the land below them into sections with the aim of supporting ground forces during their rapid advance. The East Prussian base covered Poland from the west, running as far as the Vistula, down to Grudziauz, into Warsaw then south-east to Lwow and the south-eastern regions of Poland. The Pomeranian base ran from the Polish Pomeranian frontier, east to the Vistula, and then south, encompassing Poznan, Kielce, Radom and Warsaw.

ABOVE: An exhausted soldier takes a much-needed rest during the armies' rapid advance east. He is wearing a *Feldmütze* cap and is decorated with aiguillettes, as worn by army adjutants. Normally – and certainly not under battle conditions – aiguillettes were worn purely for display purposes. For adjutants, aiguillettes were constructed in a dull silver cord and were worn nearest the right shoulder that was held in position under the right shoulder-strap by a small, grey horn button. The other end of the aiguillettes was extended across the chest and attached to the inside of the tunic.

LEFT: A German officer on horseback surveys the remains of a Polish column which has been shot up. Next to him is an antiquated World War I-era field cannon, ranked among the lightweight field cannons of its day. As it would have been in 1914, the gun was horse-drawn. For the needs of the infantry in 1939, this field cannon had an excessively great initial velocity of its shells, and the trajectory was not variable enough. Nonetheless, despite its age, firepower and design, with even a semi-trained crew the gun was still capable of seriously damaging, or even knocking out, a light tank such as the PzKpfw 1.

BELOW: Not much action for the crew of this 15cm (5.9in) sFH 18 field howitzer in an emplacement positioned prior to an artillery barrage. Everything has been unpacked and laid out, but the spade trails have not been dug in. The crew have laid some of the primed shells on the ground, which was only possible for a brief time and in dry weather. The gun pictured here was capable of firing eight different propellant charges, depending on range and effect of its desired target, but the gun's maximum range was 13,250m (14,500yd). The mats were positioned under the gun's wheels in order to prevent it from sinking.

BELOW: A column of PzKpfw 35(t)s rattles through a Polish village. This Czech-built tank was an advanced design for its day. It had an armament comparable to that of the PzKpfw III, consisting of a 3.7cm (1.45in) gun and co-axial machine gun, with a further machine gun in the front plate. It was crewed by a commander/gunner, loader, driver and hull gunner/operator. The white cross painted on the side of the turret was intended to prevent friendly fire, but became an easy aiming point for Polish antitank gunners. Gradually panzer crews painted over the cross, or painted out sections of it.

RIGHT: An army officer pulling an unusually comic face for the camera as boredom sets in on a congested road east of the Vistula in mid–September 1939. Clearly shown being worn is the officer's old style *Feldmütze*, his 6x30 binoculars, and an ammunition pouch for his pistol. Long columns of traffic like this were only possible because of overwhelming German air superiority. Freedom to move without the prospect of being attacked from the air was a main factor attributing to the fast and devastatingly effective method of *Blitzkrieg*.

ABOVE: Polish prisoners being escorted down a dirt track into captivity. Although it is very difficult to estimate just how many Poles were killed, it is known that of some 800,000 men mobilized by the Polish Government during the course of the war, a total of 694,000 were captured. The remaining 106,000 men were either killed in action, forced to flee across the border into Romania, or captured by the Red Army when it invaded on 17 September 1939.

BELOW: On the edge of a forest, the crew of a heavily camouflaged PaK 35/36 antitank gun prepare to fire its weapons. The two soldiers seen lying down as a precaution indicates the location of an enemy position; any sudden movement could attract hostile fire. Despite the armed superiority of the Germans during the campaign, the Poles were fanatical at holding their defensive positions, occasionally fighting to the death.

ABOVE: A freshly dug German soldier's grave with his M1935 helmet perched on the wooden cross as a testament to his bravery under fire. During its 36-day campaign into Poland, the German Army had lost 8082 men killed, 27, 278 wounded and 5029 missing in action. However, the casualty rate was very low indeed when compared to the Polish losses.

BELOW: Polish prisoners of war passively await instructions from their captors after their surrender. Their rifles lie in the ditch behind them. The swiftness of the German advance was a huge psychological shock to the Poles, and they did well to muster any sort of defence. Like his Polish counterpart, the German soldier fought tenaciously, making up for their inexperience with courage and zeal. There is little doubt that the German Army was a formidable opponent, its confidence enhanced and its operational techniques tried and tested. Poland was just a trial, a forerunner of larger things to come.

RIGHT: A destroyed Polish TKS tankette just outside Warsaw in late September 1939. This vehicle was probably attached to the Warsaw Mechanized Brigade which took part in the defence of the capital. The Brigade consisted of 1 7-TP tanks and 2 TKS tankette companies, of 17 and 13 vehicles per company respectively. The Germans captured an enormous amount of Polish armour and other battlefield booty. According to their count, they seized some 3214 artillery pieces, 16,500 machine guns and 1700 mortars. Although this equipment was by no means of high enough quality to fit out and restrengthen the German Army, it was nevertheless supplied to Germany's various allied satellite states.

ABOVE: Following the final defeat of Poland on 6 October 1939, a typical group of German troops have time to relax and share a joke. Two of the soldiers are wearing Polish headgear, whilst one man is dressed in a Polish Army cape with hat. Thousands of items of battlefield booty were captured by the Germans, including many discarded items of military clothing. In a number of areas, Polish troops that had become separated from their units and were aimlessly roaming the countryside for days simply deserted, throwing away their military uniforms and exchanging them for civilian clothes.

ABOVE: An unusual collection of German equipment together with some captured Polish booty appears to have been stockpiled. One probable explanation is that they have been unloaded to reequip infantry. Radio equipment, ammunition cases, Polish and German steel helmets, Mauser rifles and several MG 34 machine guns are stacked together. The MG 34 machine gun was the most powerful and effective infantry support weapon for the German soldier.

ABOVE: The end finally comes to some of the last remnants of the Polish Army here being rounded up and sent to the rear as PoWs. Both Paris and London were amazed by the success of a style of warfare that had cost the Germans no more than one per cent of their army in order to overrun half of Poland in less than four weeks. Although the Polish Army were badly led, with antiquated equipment and supplies, as a whole it was a brave force and fought exceptionally well against the weight of the *Wehrmacht* and later the Red Army. By 18 September, its survivors were trapped inside a gigantic double pincer.

CHAPTER THREE

The Western Campaign

The Low Countries Attacked

The destructive embrace of the lightning war against Poland forced the West to concede that the *Blitzkrieg* tactics employed by the *Wehrmacht* were the daredevil capabilities of a modern, fully equipped army. It revealed to both Britain and France how, by using speed and the destructiveness of German ground and air operations, rapid victories could be attained. *Blitzkrieg* had befallen Poland. As far as Hitler was concerned, these tactics were only the beginning. In a Führer directive for a western offensive, he outlined his plan for exactly how that destruction would be achieved. The purpose of the offensive, as stated in his directive, was to defeat the French Army and the forces of the Allies fighting on their side, wherever possible. At the same time, the Germans would win territories in Holland, Belgium and northern France which were to serve as bases for the successful implementation of the air war against England. The planned attack in the West was immediately drawn up in early October 1939, but it was not until the spring of 1940 that it finally got the go ahead.

ACHTUNG PANZER

During the afternoon of 9 May 1940, Hitler finally set out the signal to all units that were poised to take part in the German offensive in the West. By late evening, the codeword 'Danzig!' alerted them that the word for action had finally arrived, that they were now to 'Go!' The key objective for the rapid success of the operation was the use of the panzer units of Army Group A, which were going to strike south through Luxembourg and the wooded terrain of the Ardennes which, up to then, had been regarded as impassable for armour. In the northern sector, Army Group B concentrated the main weight of the offensive in through Belgium, which was designed to lure the Allies into a trap. It was here that the British Expeditionary Force (BEF), together with the French and Belgian Army, expected to meet the main forces of the *Wehrmacht* moving westwards.

Early on 10 May, the invasion of the Low Countries began. Initial air attacks paralysed enemy defences along the Dutch and Belgian frontier. Minutes later, *Fallschirmjäger* forces began massive glider- and parachute assaults with a series of key objectives. They were to capture strategically important bridges and airfields. These 2000 highly trained and well-equipped troops of the German 7th Air Division and 12,000 troops of the 22nd Airborne Division were also assigned other special tasks that included attacking and securing key airfields and bridges around cities such as Amsterdam, Utrecht, Rotterdam and Dordrecht. Apart from reaching these targets, they were also assigned the objective of destroying or capturing the High Command, which at that point was situated at The Hague. In Belgium, the *Fallschirmjäger* men were set a number of immense and risky challenges, which included not only the destruction of a string of heavily armoured fortifications along the frontier, but also the annihilation of one of the most formidable fortifications in the world, as yet untouched: Eben Emael.

ABOVE: Among the rubble of a building, two French Hotchkiss H-35 tanks have been knocked out by air attack inside a Belgian town. The French Army had some 3132 modern tanks on 10 May 1940, and about 550 new tanks were brought in to replace the losses which would be sustained in the battles to come. Although the Hotchkiss H-35 tank had thicker armour than that of their German opponents, its speed was lower and the radius of action limited. The available armour for both the French and BEF forces was not inferior to the quantity – about 3500 for each side – nor was it inferior in quality when compared to the panzers. However, its outdated Allied tank tactics made it inferior and doomed to certain destruction.

By 11 May, following a bitter and bloody battle, the paratroopers had cracked the Belgian defence and seized the strongest fortification in the world. The operation was without doubt daring and decisive, and played a key role in the *Blitzkrieg*. The *Luftwaffe* too continued in its dominant role of preparing the ground offensive, and was able to put into action some 3634 front-line aircraft, of which 1016 were fighters, and the rest, 1562, bombers. This was the key to success in the Low Countries, and this immediately became apparent when the ground forces of Army Group B, under the command of General von Bock, began its lightning attack.

For the attack against the West, the offensive was divided into two army groups. Army Group B was given the task of pushing its troops and fast-moving armoured columns through Belgium and Holland. Army Group A, commanded by Field Marshal Gerd von Rundstedt, was given the task of sweeping through the Ardennes, and surprising the Allies in northern France with its powerful panzer divisions. In total, both groups had 134 divisions deployed facing Belgium, Holland, Luxembourg and France. Among these were 10 panzer divisions, a strength of some 2771 panzers. Army Group A consisted of 45 divisions, of which 7 were panzers. Army Group B consisted of 29 divisions, of which there were 3 panzer divisions. Although the main concentration of armour was deployed in the south through the Ardennes, the three panzer divisions were supported by almost the entire German airborne force.

ATTACKING HOLLAND

The ground attack through the Low Countries was conducted by the Eighteenth Army under General George von Küchler, which unleashed a furious three-pronged assault. Although the Eighteenth Army was smaller than that of the Dutch Army it faced, within hours of the first pulverizing attacks, it was busily overwhelming the bulk of Dutch resistance.

However, in a number of areas, the planned attack did not go according to plan. Some Dutch fortifications put up stiff resistance, and German heavy artillery was called up. On the Maas River at Gennep, the 9th Panzer Division invaded the Netherlands, brushed remnants of the French Ninth Army to one side, and crossed the Moerdijk bridges, which had been captured intact by the *Fallschirmjäger*. French forces were further harassed by heavy ground- and air attacks and compelled, along with the Dutch forces, to withdraw in disorder back towards Antwerp. In the Low

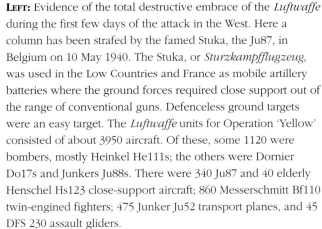

LEFT: Evidence of the total destructive embrace of the *Luftwaffe* during the first few days of the attack in the West. Here a column has been strafed by the famed Stuka, the Ju87, in Belgium on 10 May 1940. The Stuka, or *Sturzkampfflugzeug*, was used in the Low Countries and France as mobile artillery batteries where the ground forces required close support out of the range of conventional guns. Defenceless ground targets were an easy target. The *Luftwaffe* units for Operation 'Yellow' consisted of about 3950 aircraft. Of these, some 1120 were bombers, mostly Heinkel He111s; the others were Dornier Do17s and Junkers Ju88s. There were 340 Ju87 and 40 elderly Henschel Hs123 close-support aircraft; 860 Messerschmitt Bf110 twin-engined fighters; 475 Junker Ju52 transport planes, and 45 DFS 230 assault gliders.

Countries, German soldiers quickly discovered what infantry and metal alone could achieve. Their rapid advance took them head-on into huge, retreating enemy formations, and brought them the capture of town after town, village after village. Rotterdam was within sight; its capture would provide a victory in Fortress Holland. By 13 May the 9th Panzer Division finally arrived on the outskirts of Rotterdam. The Dutch, however, still held most of the city, but following a massive air raid centred on the bridgehead, Rotterdam finally surrendered on 15 May, along with shattered remnants of the entire Dutch Army.

BELGIUM INVADED

While the 9th Panzer Division advanced on Rotterdam, two panzer divisions allotted to the Sixth Army simultaneously attacked through the narrow strip of land which separates Germany, Holland and Belgium. These forces were part of General Erich Höpner's XVI Panzer Corps and were heading in the direction of the Belgian city of Maastricht. The destruction of the Meuse bridges at Masstricht had provided the Belgian Army with some respite, but by the afternoon of 11 May the first panzer divisions began crossing the Meuse on pontoons. Later that day, a portable bridge was slung over the river to allow the rest of the mighty XVI Panzer Corps to cross. The Belgian Army had regarded the rivers and canals as a major obstacle to the German motorized units and was sure it would further limit their advance. But the panzers still proved adept at negotiating the water obstacles, even when heavily defended, and the Belgian forces soon found

LEFT: A Horch light staff car has not been hit by enemy fire, but its engine compartment appears to have spontaneously ignited and burst into flames. The driver is hastily salvaging all he can muster before the car is completely engulfed. Engine fires on Horch light staff cars were common to this particular make of vehicle. In fact, a Horch vehicle temporarily used a year later by General Erwin Rommel in Africa suddenly developed engine mechanical failure and burst into flames.

themselves outflanked on the Albert Canal by the thundering 4th Panzer Division. On the Meuse, the 3rd and 4th Panzer Divisions unleashed their armoured vehicles across the river while the Royal Air Force tried in vain, in a series of suicidal bombing missions, to destroy the bridges across the Meuse in the face of the German advance. The Belgian Army, however, continued to withdraw, hoping that the French First Army and the BEF behind them would support their dwindling ranks on the Dyle. However, the French First Army had only two cavalry divisions and the British hardly any armour at all. Confronting them was Höpner's armoured corps, consisting of the 3rd and 4th Panzer Divisions with some 600 tanks. Its panzer crews were battle-hardened veterans of the last *Blitzkrieg* attack on Poland and were now determined to give the Allies a taste of death in Flanders.

As the entire front started to crumble in indecision and confusion, the men of the demoralized French Army tended to their wounds and withdrew to Antwerp. A potential disaster now loomed for the Allies, as it had in 1914, but the crisis this time was potentially far worse. On the BEF front lines, there was chaos. Units were becoming trapped, captured, overrun and slaughtered. The British were now seriously confronted by the fear of losing their only army, and large parts of their air force, if they continued to stand by the French and Belgians on the collapsing line. Meanwhile the French, too, were under incredible pressure and were also compelled to take immediate action before becoming cut off and destroyed. Totally demoralized and downcast, their men reluctantly retreated further west, and soon found themselves back on French soil.

BELOW: Captured French soldiers tending to their wounded following the successful breakthrough of German armour west of the Meuse on 15 May 1940. Both Dutch and Belgian forces were badly shaken by the fury of the German armoured assault. Meanwhile the French First, Seventh, and Ninth Armies, along with the BEF, put into action its Dyle Plan for the defence of the Low Countries. They were sited along the Dyle and Meuse river line in Belgium. However, the Allies had totally underestimated their opponents, and were either ground down in a battle of attrition, forced to retreat, or encircled and destroyed.

ABOVE: Captured BEF troops being marched into captivity. Facing the first phase of the German invasion was the 51st Highland Division, which was attached to the French Third Army defending the Maginot Line, and the 12th, 23rd, and 46th Territorial Divisions, which were assigned to labouring duties in the rear due to lack of equipment. These soldiers were no match against the superior fighting quality of the German Army. Not only were they faced with well-equipped and trained troops, but they were also surprised by the panzer divisions' lightning strike that had literally ripped through their defences.

BELOW: A precarious crossing by the gun crew of this 15cm (5.9in) sFH 18 field howitzer as it ferries its weapon across the Meuse on 12 May 1940. Because of the weight and size of the gun, it is being transported in two pieces. The barrel trailer or 'barrel cart' was positioned low, almost right over the trailer axle, and was drawn back only far enough to maintain the trailer's centre of gravity. The technique of moving the gun in two parts was always considered difficult, and invariably consumed a lot of time, especially when a crew was trying to keep up with the advanced armoured spearheads.

LEFT: In a drastic attempt to contain the armoured spearheads of the panzer divisions and prevent them from crossing the Meuse, the French, Belgians and BEF blew a number of bridges across it. For this reason, the construction of pontoon bridges was widely used in Belgium by German bridge-building units. A number of commanders had become so impatient to get across the Meuse and continue their rapid advance that they drove heavy tanks – such as the PzKpfw IV – onto pontoon rafts that exceeded the latter's weight limit by more than 100 per cent. On occasions this would prove fatal, sending the raft and tank crew to the bottom of the river.

ABOVE: Captured battlefield booty in a field in Belgium. Hundreds of French and Belgian steel helmets and other souvenirs of war lie as reminders of the cost of defending the Low Countries against the Germans. In the background captured armour has been draped with a canvas sheet in order to conceal it from enemy aerial observation. A number of captured French tanks were repainted and given a new tactical number before being sent into battle again on the German side.

ABOVE: Hundreds of French and colonial troops have been captured, including soldiers of the 4th African Division. With no German transport available to move them, they are compelled to march on foot to the German rear. With the Meuse breached in many places, the French and BEF had failed to press home any meaningful assault. Consequently this allowed the enemy to assemble and launch a series of concerted attacks to expand his bridgehead and bypass and encircle more enemy forces. The consequences of these manoeuvres for the Allies is shown in this photograph.

71

ABOVE: The face of *Blitzkrieg*. A PzKpfw IV races down a French road, the tank's commander standing in his turret. He holds in his hand a baton to give signals to other panzers, used like semaphore flags. Using the baton allows the panzers to operate in radio silence. The PzKpfw IV was armed with a low-velocity 7.5cm (2.95in) gun which was capable of knocking out most potential opposition. However the tank was not as heavily armoured as some of its Allied opponents. Nonetheless the PzKpfw IV was a good all-round tank design, and in various guises it remained in service throughout the war.

RIGHT: It was difficult to negotiate the sometimes-narrow congested roads through Belgium. As a consequence, vehicles occasionally fell into ditches by the roadside or became stuck in the soil while attempting to pass a larger vehicle. In this photograph troops are trying to move a truck using pieces of wood under its front wheels. Judging by the speed of one of the soldiers, it appears that it urgently needs to be removed, as it could be causing a serious traffic jam. Note the old man and two children in the nearby field watching the Germans struggle with the vehicle.

BELOW: A soldier peers into the hatch of an abandoned British Mk VI light tank. The tank was more than likely attached to the 1st Armoured Division which totalled some 174 Mk IV light Cruiser tanks equipped with a two-pounder. In total the BEF had some 300 tanks in France, around 200 being VIB light cavalry tanks, whilst the others consisted of infantry tanks. Of these, 77 were Matildas Is armed only with a machine gun, and only 23 of them were the modern Matilda II type.

ABOVE: A knocked-out SdKfz 263. This radio vehicle, which was equipped with a long-range radio set and usually used in signals units, has received a direct hit on its engine at the front. The impact of the enemy shell has blown one of its wheels clean off, leaving the front wheels charred and with no tyres. The extent of the fire damage to this SdKfz 263 indicates that the entire inside may have been gutted, rendering the salvage of its radio equipment impossible.

LEFT: Another view of the same abandoned Vickers Mk VI light tank seen on the previous page. The vehicle had a three-man crew and weighed some 5.2 tonnes (5.7 tons). It was armed with a 12.7mm (0.5in) machine gun and a 7.7mm (0.303in); an armament which proved not to be very effective, even when it was directed against the lightly-armoured PzKpfw I. Although the speed of this vehicle and its reliability compensated somewhat for its poor armour and firepower, in Belgium and France the Mk VI tank proved to be of limited combat value, even in the reconnaissance role.

ABOVE: A group of soldiers from an unidentified regiment bury some of their comrades killed in action in Belgium. The *Blitzkrieg* campaign to capture the Low Countries and then France was more costly to the Germans than that to take Poland. In total there were at least 200,000 casualties, of whom 40,000 died. Although there is no accurate German figure of how many soldiers were killed during their rapid advance through Belgium, it is estimated than more than 5000 were mortally wounded. This would have been regarded by the German High Command as a light loss, considering the huge array of forces that had been assigned to the campaign.

BELOW: The attacks across the Meuse were preceded and accompanied by a series of heavy, sustained bombardments of enemy defensive positions by the *Luftwaffe*. During this period, the bulk of the German artillery was still struggling through the Ardennes, trying to make its way to the front lines. For nearly 10 hours the *Luftwaffe* mercilessly pounded French positions. In this photograph, a German soldier scours the west bank of the Meuse, which is still burning during the night following a heavy attack in the day. The French men defending this position must have been subjected to a long and demoralizing attack that caused an unprecedented amount of casualties.

ABOVE: A crew member of a 15cm (5.9in) sFH 18 heavy field howitzer sits under the camouflage netting with his gun. The sheer power of this weapon could hurl its destructive charge to a maximum range of 13,250m (14,500yd). As the standard German heavy field howitzer during the *Blitzkrieg* in the west, the gun was very effective at clearing heavily concentrated enemy defensive positions. Its high muzzle velocity and weighty shell made it absolutely lethal. Although a very heavy weapon – especially with a split-trail carriage of some 5512kg (12,154lb) – by the time it was employed in action against the West, much of its transportation was done by half-track instead of horse. This enabled the crews to work much quicker and minimized the distance between artillery and advanced elements of the panzer units.

BELOW: A dismounted motorcyclist watches a Renault FT tank burn after it apparently received a direct hit from antitank fire, probably from a PaK 35/36 antitank gun. These tanks were antiquated and dated back from World War I. Amazingly, 1500 were still serviceable by May 1940, but they were no match against the superior German panzer designs. Being handicapped by a poor main gun, and slow, they were much easier targets than the Renault R35 or the Char B1 *bis* tanks.

LEFT: Advancing west through Belgium is a column of German troops, with a variety of vehicles and horse-drawn transport pulling artillery. Long unopposed marches like these were common in Belgium; the Allies used outdated tactics, and units moving up to try to retrieve the situation were dissipated along the defence line or sent to plug huge gaps made by the panzer divisions. With armoured units sometimes as far as 16–24km (10–15 miles) ahead, Germans seldom encountered the enemy, but would pass the devastation already wrought on him by the panzers and *Luftwaffe*.

BELOW: German infantry take a much-needed rest behind a wall. These soldiers are attached to the 4th Panzer Division. Having already crossed the Meuse and Albert Canal in southern Holland, they attacked Belgian formations in the Liege area. Note the two radio operators kneeling among two of their comrades. Attached to their M1935 steel helmets is foliage which is being held in place by rubber rings. Individuals sometimes utilized various other bits of material around their helmets to keep foliage in place, including elasticated rings, cloth rags, and chicken-wire mesh.

ABOVE: More BEF, French, and colonial troops pass by in a long, dejected column following days of punishing *Luftwaffe* attacks and pulverizing armoured penetrations. A number of these prisoners are probably French tank crews. Severe logistical difficulties in Belgium had resulted in many French tanks running out of fuel before they could reach the battle area. This consequently left many of their crews abandoned and easy prey to the advancing German armour.

LEFT: Soldiers on bicycles ride along another congested Belgian road, while refugees flee from the fighting. These German cyclists are carrying all the provisions they might need in order to sustain them on the battlefield. The troops have travelled by bicycle all the way from Holland, a journey made possible due to the miles and miles of flat terrain found in the Low Countries. Ammunition boxes can be seen strapped to the back of their cycles over the wheel, and each man is wearing the basic kit of a German soldier, including gas-mask canister, rolled-up *Zeltbahn*, entrenching tool, and M98 rifles.

ABOVE: A 14.5-tonne (16-ton) pontoon bridge that has been erected across the Meuse to allow the mass of German armour to pour across and continue its mighty spearhead west. These vehicles – medium cross-country Horch cars and Opel medium trucks – are following in the wake of the armoured drive. Despite the shortages of vehicles in the *Wehrmacht*, during this period of the war there were no less than 100 different types of commercial lorries in army service. Many, some of which were civilian vehicles kept in reserve, were flimsy by design and outdated by the time the invasion of the West had begun. Hundreds proved to be unreliable and as a consequence were replaced by horse-drawn transport.

ABOVE: Pausing to take stock during their furious advance; panzer crews have a chance of rest in the line. One crew member jokes with his comrades and dons a British black bowler hat to ridicule his enemy's retreat into France. It can be clearly recognized that when dismounted, these black panzer uniforms offer little in the way of concealment. It is also interesting to note that these men are not wearing the standard black field cap, but grey M1938 *Feldmütze* caps worn by the regular army. The special black panzer uniform was the same design and colouring for all ranks of the panzer arm, including generals of the *Panzertruppen*, apart from rank insignia.

ABOVE: French and colonial troops are being marched to the rear following overwhelming German superiority in Belgium. When these troops had been lured deep into Belgium, their commanders had no idea whether the force would meet entrenched infantry, antitank guns, tanks or merely soft transport. So naïve were their commanders, they had ordered the attack without proper reconnaissance. The consequences were enormous. Within hours of the first punishing strikes, the troops were overwhelmed against powerful armour, coupled with the deadly blows of the *Luftwaffe* that wreaked havoc on enemy columns, causing unprecedented destruction on the front lines. Fast and devastating *Blitzkrieg* had arrived.

ABOVE: Belgian refugees pass an SdKfz 8 prime-mover towing a partly camouflaged 15cm (5.9in) sFH 18 heavy field howitzer. For the immediate needs of battle, the panzer divisions took their artillery with them. Each panzer division had three battalions of artillery; the heavy battalion had 12 sFH 18 howitzers. The sheer weight of these artillery pieces and the way in which they had to be towed and positioned in the field was more than reason enough why artillery needed tracked vehicles, rather than slow, cumbersome horse-drawn transport. In 1940, half-tracks were the backbone of the *Wehrmacht* for the task of towing artillery to the front lines.

BELOW: Officers, NCOs and their men during a lull in the fighting inside a Belgian town near the French border. They are wearing their M1935 steel helmets, indicating that they may be still embroiled in fighting in the area. The service tunic worn by army officers was usually better quality material and had the noticeable difference of plain, deep turn-back cuffs. The officer's service tunic was worn with trousers and lace-up ankle shoes or, as was usually the case, with officers' breeches and high riding boots. Officers had a choice of head-dress to be worn with the service uniform: the uniform cap, the officers field service cap, or the steel helmet.

BELOW: A Horch heavy cross-country car is about to cross a damaged bridge that the retreating enemy has failed to destroy. In the Low Countries, the Dutch, then the Belgians, along with the French and BEF forces, had tried frantically to impede the mighty German armoured advance by blowing up as many river crossings as possible. The Allies used the waterways as a defence line in the face of an attack. Blowing the bridges was not only an attempt to delay the Germans as long as possible along the axis of their withdrawal; it also served to warn the area of the Germans' approach. However, in both Holland and Belgium, the *Fallschirmjäger* (German paratroopers) managed to secure a number of important bridges in order to allow the panzer divisions to cross without delay and push forward in order to secure their tactical objectives.

RIGHT: A soldier has been badly wounded in action and his comrades appear to be waiting for medical support. They are all wearing the M1938 *Feldmütze* apart from one soldier standing on the left who wears a M1935 steel helmet. Note on the side of his helmet is the tricolour shield displaying the national colours of black, white and red. On the left of his helmet would be a silver-white 'Wehrmachtadler' (army eagle) on a black shield. During 1940 the tricolour shield on the helmet was phased out, followed later by the *Wehrmacht*-style eagle and swastika.

ABOVE: German infantry following in the wake of the armoured spearhead through Belgium. The infantry were trained to carry out many simple engineering tasks. Inflatable boats were supplied right down to company level, while the infantry battalion had pontoons and trestles that could put together to make a 4.5-tonne (5-ton) bridge. To ferry men and equipment, the soldiers here have used inflatable boats more than capable of carrying antitank guns or the small infantry howitzer. Soldiers can be seen handling a cart packed full of supplies that has been unhitched from the horses on the far bank of the river.

RIGHT: A general standing next to his Horch light staff car reads some papers. This vehicle was more than likely fitted with an early-pattern general's vehicle pennant on the right mudguard, and a panzer group commander's command flag on the left mudguard beside the engine compartment, as well as on the front bumper. The Horch light staff cars were mainly painted a standard colour, using dark grey paint. For *Wehrmacht* identification purposes, they would probably have displayed the first letter of the commander's name in white on their front- or rear mudguard.

BELOW: The ravages of war were an all too familiar sight to the soldiers advancing across the Belgian countryside. In this photograph, behind the wreckage of a strafed enemy column, German horse-drawn transport trudges slowly past, towing artillery towards the French frontier. An ordinary German infantry division of this period had 5375 horses, an immense amount considering they consumed over 45.3 tonnes (50 tons) of hay and oats a day. Horses demanded much manpower, for they had to be constantly watered, cleaned, fed, and exercised. Their harnesses and other equipment also had to be checked daily, and there had to be a round-the-clock back-up of health checks and veterinary care for both sick and healthy animals.

ABOVE: A column of horse-drawn transport – most belonging to a field kitchen unit attached to one of the advancing columns – makes its way across a recently-constructed wooden framed bridge in Belgium. The blown bridge next to the column does not appear to have hindered the drive in any way. German pioneer units were well-practiced in constructing pontoon bridges as rapidly as possible. The mass deployment of horses was obviously not considered an effective weapon of *Blitzkrieg*, but with the shortages of motor vehicles, relatively low-priority units such as field kitchens were transported by horse and cart rather than half-tracks.

ABOVE: Soldiers sift through a huge stockpile of French and Belgian battlefield booty. The Germans were masters at salvaging what they could find and would re-use a number of various captured French and British weapons, since the French equipment proved to be equal and even superior to that of the Germans. Various tanks too – like the French Char B1, Somula 35, and the Renault R35 – were just a few of the vehicles pressed back into service with the *Wehrmacht*. In some cases, captured French crews were even ordered by their enemies to drive these tanks through France.

ABOVE: A motorcyclist accompanies a Horch staff car as it crosses the French border. In the summer of 1940 there were two main motorcycles, mass-produced for the *Wehrmacht* by BMW and Zundapp. Both of these companies were in a hurry to manufacture powerful 750cc motorcycle combinations with engines that drove the rear wheel of the bike as well as the sidecar wheels. Although the *Wehrmacht* put hundreds of soldiers on motorcycles, motorcycles were quite unsuited to modern war, except as despatch riders. On bad road surfaces they were totally useless, and riders were vulnerable to small-arms fire and mantraps. But thanks to the exceptionally fine weather that summer, there were few impassable roads.

RIGHT: Bewildered French civilians watch as a column of Horch medium cross-country cars pass a French border point. With buildings and roads still intact, there appear to be no signs of defensive action in this area, suggesting that the BEF and French forces had withdrawn very quickly along this frontier to escape the German spearheads. In the north the German armoured forces crossed the French frontier and moved along the northern side of the River Somme. The river provided adequate protection against French counterattacks.

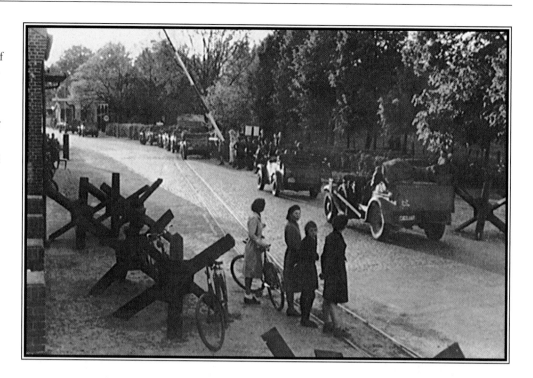

ABOVE: Under a freak downpour just across the French border in the north of the country, German troops frantically try to pull a horse-drawn cart out of the mud. Soldiers who had to endure it frowned on this type of weather. In this sector, it rained incessantly, halting the horse-drawn transport that the Germans relied on for supplies. The horse's heart was heavily strained through pulling the immobilized cart; later, on the Eastern Front, hundreds would perish through heart failure.

LEFT: A chance to relax in the sun and play cards while their unit prepares to move out into France. In some assembly areas before the last phase of the campaign in France, there was a feeling of widespread relief among the troops. At last they were about to begin the final battle on which all their thoughts had been focused for so long. Any fears were overcome by excitement at the feeling that they were élite. Other men, however, felt more compelled during the invasion of France than exhilarated by it, but for most troops, this was an historic moment and one in which they were more than happy to play a part.

ABOVE: More troops in the same assembly area waiting to move off into France. Here the soldiers are taking advantage of the presence of the local livestock by milking a Belgian cow. Fresh milk was something of a rarity to the soldiers. Field kitchens were an important part of the soldiers' lives, and many studies have shown the necessity of regular hot meals to maintain soldiers' morale. Although German supply lines became strained, they did not break down, unlike those of the Allies.

CHAPTER FOUR

The Road to Dunkirk

The Allies Collapse

As in 1914, Allied intelligence had failed to establish where the main German attack would come in 1940. In 1914 the French expected the attack to come through the wooded terrain of the Ardennes, but its forces should have been ready for battle in Flanders. Twenty-six years later, the Allied air forces flew across Flanders fields, when they should have been flying over the Ardennes.

It was here in the south that Rundstedt's forces of Army Group A, consisting of seven panzer divisions, quickly and decisively broke through the wooded terrain of the Ardennes which, up to then, had been regarded as impassable for armour. Through the narrow, twisting lanes, between steep slopes and over many humpback bridges, cut by streams, columns of panzers and other motorized vehicles rattled across the Belgian, Luxembourg and French borders. Rolling through villages, tank men smiled and waved to amazed civilians from their open turrets. Using the roads was more a matter of traffic control than actual fighting, and one breakdown of one large vehicle might have been enough to bring the invasion in the south to a standstill. But the flat land beyond was a tank commander's dream. With wide-open plains stretched out before them, panzers would be able to make a grand northward sweep through France towards the Channel coast, thus cutting the Anglo–French armies in two.

THROUGH THE ARDENNES

For four days between 10 and 14 May 1940, hundreds of vehicles advanced nose-to-tail through the Ardennes. Over 800 panzers were deployed among the 7 panzer divisions. A great procession of tanks, artillery, trucks and other armoured vehicles rolled along the narrow roads. In endless lines, the convoys roared through, heading west

LEFT: A Hotchkiss H-39 tank has received a hit from antitank fire and lies knocked out on a Belgian road near the French border. There were about 370 Hotchkiss tanks in the French Army.
FAR LEFT: Near Flavion, where members of the 4th North Africa Division had been captured while preparing for a new defence line, a colonial soldier sits by the road and eats bread, waiting to be taken to the rear as a PoW.

towards the Meuse. No one was permitted to stop; troops stood everywhere to keep the traffic flowing. For the drivers, there was no reason to stop; in most places the drive was going well. In just a few hours Rundstedt's forces had catapulted across the frontier and burst through the Ardennes, surprising Belgian and French forces. As the first day drew to a close, although the panzer divisions had made good progress, the von Kleist Group had failed to reach its objectives. During the night, however, it had caught up with its tight timetable, and had successfully driven back French cavalry units.

Within 24 hours of the initial attack, the French military situation was already worsening. Under extreme pressure from advancing enemy armour, units were being ordered back behind the Meuse. Those forces that were either cut off or unable to get back across the river were compelled to meet the fury of the German advance. The quality of the German weapons – above all tanks – was of immense importance for the rapid speed of gaining ground. The attack through the Ardennes was a product of dazzling organization and staff work, and great technical ingenuity. The advance had been so rapid that the bulk of the artillery and infantry were left far behind, and supply units became strained because of the overwhelming extended lines. But Rundstedt was also determined to keep the element of surprise to the utmost, without waiting for the necessary reinforcements that were tailing back far in the rear. He stated that the strategy of Operation 'Yellow' was to continue to press on regardless and keep the momentum of speed alive, which was the most important ingredient of *Blitzkrieg*. The Allies had no real concept of the tactics of *Blitzkrieg* and made no real effort to hasten reinforcements in front of the thundering panzers. All that was now required of Army Group A was to cross the Meuse and advance across the flat, open terrain north through France.

CROSSING THE MEUSE

By 13 May, German armoured units had arrived at the Meuse and were already preparing to cross. The success of this crossing was crucial to the German drive into France. Nothing was more dangerous for an army than to cross a river, especially when the enemy opposed its banks. The first of Rundstedt's forces to arrive at the Meuse was that of General Erwin Rommel's 7th Panzer Division. Rommel's light division had not plunged its forces through the deep forests; he had avoided this type of terrain and skirted around the dense undergrowth to reach the river. His division was one of the most powerful panzer divisions in the field. Commanding a tank unit for the first time was a proud and exhilarating venture for Rommel. At only 48

years old, he would soon master the complexities of his new command, and in France would reveal to the world that he had became the greatest and most famous *Blitzkrieg* tactician of World War II.

The first element of Rommel's division to arrive at the Meuse was a motorcycle unit near Dinant. Further upriver it attempted to cross, but came under intense French fire. During the night, armed with MG 34s, the motorcycle unit managed to get across and drive the French infantry regiment from its meagre position on the west bank. And so the first Germans were across the Meuse. In a number of areas where the French could not use the river as a defence line, their forces were compelled to slowly withdraw. Shortages of antitank guns and armour made it more difficult to consolidate their position, especially when German tanks and artillery support were ordered across the Meuse.

By dawn on 14 May, pontoon bridges were constructed; cable ferries also began transporting armour and infantry across, and even inflatable boats were pressed into service. Along some parts of the Meuse the Germans met spirited resistance, but that was either destroyed or bypassed. The crossing of the Meuse enabled the panzer divisions of Army Group A to drive with all its fury northwards towards the Channel coast and wreak

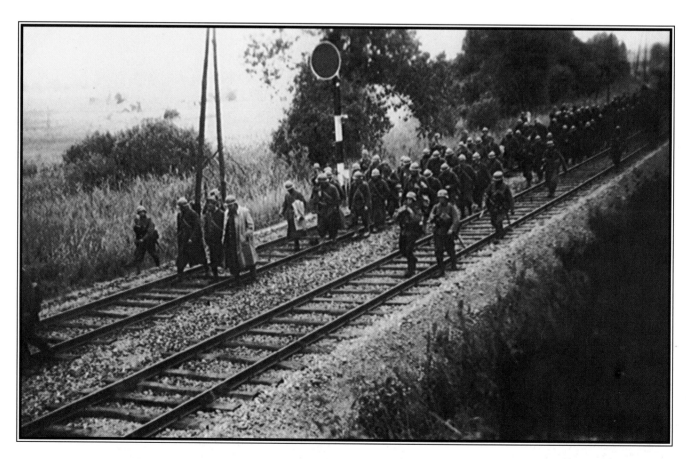

ABOVE: Using one of the easiest forms of avoiding the congestion on the clogged roads running through Belgium and France, captured French prisoners are being marched to the rear along a railway line just across the French border on 21 May 1940. The French soldiers at the front of this dejected column appear to be commanding officers.

ABOVE: What appears to be a Renault/AMX UE tractor being pressed into service by the Germans in northern France. This vehicle was normally operated by a crew of two men and was equipped with a large, open tray in the rear for carrying a load. These vehicles would prove to be reliable during the French campaign and, since they had excellent cross-country capabilities, hundreds of them were soon incorporated into the *Wehrmacht*. A year later, in 1941, they were designated UE 630(f) and were widely utilized at the Eastern Front in Russia for a variety of purposes.

BELOW: Captured French prisoners being led away past a group of soldiers from a German artillery regiment after being captured by General Heinz Guderian's panzer corps. On 21 May 1940, after Guderian's panzers secured a bridgehead on the Somme, he advanced at speed on Boulogne and Calais. These captured troops are probably from the French Third Army Group on the Somme that was still trying to build up a new front with the Sixth and Seventh Armies. General Besson, commander of the French Third Army, had less than half of his original equipment to use against the mighty panzer divisions.

ABOVE: French buildings have been destroyed following intense attacks by the German armoured spearheads. By 21 May German armour had demonstrated its ability to penetrate enemy lines, all the while bypassing strongpoints and holding the enemy at bay until their own lines of communication could be restored. For the defenders trying to hold onto important parts of the front line, the situation steadily grew worse, and the death toll amongst their men rose dramatically.

disaster on the remnants of the BEF and French forces. Victory was now within its grasp. Operation 'Red', the battle for France, had begun.

SWEEPING INTO FRANCE

On 18 May, General Heinz Guderian's reconnaissance crossed the River Somme and captured Peronne. Panzers swept on into France, even stopping to fill up at public petrol stations when they outstripped supply facilities. Masses of French troops that had not already been killed or injured were persuaded to surrender. The Germans used nothing more than orders shouted from the turrets of passing tanks to coerce these French troops. Once, when several French tanks were captured, Rommel incorporated them into his own column, still with their French drivers. Not all the French soldiers resisted so lightly. In areas in the north of the country, they resisted steadily, until finally the French First Army and the BEF were constricted between the North Sea and the advancing panzers.

By 20 May, after racing north along the Somme against fierce resistance from the British 12th and 23rd Territorial Divisions, the first panzers came into sight of the Channel. In no more than 11 days, Guderian and his force had advanced some 644km (400 miles) and done what the German Army had failed to accomplish in four years during World War I. It seemed that nothing on earth could stop this stampede of military might from crushing the Anglo-French troops that were being driven along the Channel coast.

However, as plans were put forward by Guderian to move his 10th Panzer Division on the port of Dunkirk – where it was believed there was a considerable number of isolated enemy troops – General Kleist removed Guderian's 10th Panzer and ordered him to capture Boulogne instead with the 2nd Panzer Division. His 1st Panzer Division was to attack Calais. By nightfall of 22 May, Guderian's 2nd Panzer Division, after a drive of more than 64km (40 miles), arrived on the outskirts of Boulogne. As German troops and armour closed in to secure the port,

RIGHT: Four German soldiers march a worried French infantryman through a village in northern France. The French Army was at a huge disadvantage when the Germans rode into France. It was led by high-ranking officers who, although experienced veterans of World War I, seemed ready to re-fight the last war instead of adapting their tactics to the new equipment available. As a consequence, the Germans were able to employ their modern *Blitzkrieg* tactics successfully, outflanking or trapping large numbers of the enemy in pockets as they pushed forward.

panic-stricken British soldiers fled into the sea in a drastic attempt to get away to England by boat. Further up the coast, in the Stuka-battered town of Calais, the situation for the BEF was equally as dire and dismal. The bravery shown by the British 30th Brigade in defending the port was said by the attacking German troops to be nothing but a useless sacrifice.

DUNKIRK

As disaster loomed in France for the entire Anglo-French armies, it was becoming clear to the British that their hopes would rest entirely on Dunkirk and its beaches. For a number of days, thousands of exhausted, dishevelled troops with a large assortment of vehicles, ranging from armoured cars to ambulances, swarmed through Dunkirk and on to the beach. Relations in Dunkirk between the Allies were already strained. The British were more concerned about evacuation, but the French regarded the port as a fortress, a base from which to launch the counterattack that would somehow undermine the German thrust into France.

Inside the bombed and blasted town, a swirling mass of despondent men with their horses and guns clogged the streets leading to the beach. Their retreat to the sandy shores of the Channel coast had been a nightmare. Many of them they were lucky to have escaped from the clutches of the German drive. Dazed and disorganized, the soldiers were crammed onto the beach, hoping that evacuation from the sea would come at any moment. As the BEF waited to be evacuated, Guderian's 1st Panzer Division, which was racing towards Dunkirk, reached the Aa Canal between Holque and the coast, and secured bridgeheads across it.

On 24 May, with just a few miles to cover before reaching Dunkirk, Guderian suddenly received a startling order from Hitler. It instructed him to halt operations towards Dunkirk: the tanks were to stand west of the canal line. The *Luftwaffe* was given the task of breaking the resistance from the encircled enemy and preventing them escaping across the Channel. Outside Dunkirk, Guderian and other bewildered commanders found it difficult to come to terms with the halt order.

Although there was widespread feeling of uncertainty in the German High Command about committing armour into what Hitler remembered from his own experiences of World War I as 'the marshy plains of Flanders', there was also a political motivation. According to Field Marshal von Manstein, Hitler had wanted a compromise peace with the British, which would not be possible if he destroyed their army. The Field Marshal also provided two other explanations for the halt order. Firstly, the Führer was eager to keep his armour intact for the coming battle in central France, and secondly he thought it was Göring's turn to use his *Luftwaffe* to gain victory for his airmen.

Thus, with the panzers growling outside Dunkirk, hundreds of vessels sailed across the turbulent Channel waters to evacuate more than 300,000 men. Despite heavy, sometimes sustained, Luftwaffe attacks, soldiers continued to leave the bomb-cratered beach by boat. On 4 June, the thin perimeter of the Dunkirk defence line finally burst, and as the last troops wearily clambered on board a packed ship bound for England, the sound of German machine-gun fire could be heard crackling in the streets of the town. With the British more or less defeated, a confident Hitler now ordered that the bulk of his forces move swiftly to take Paris.

ABOVE: Inside the French town of Abbeville following its capture, a group of German infantrymen gather along a road. These soldiers are more than likely part of the 2nd Panzer Division, as they were given the objective of cutting through the British lines and reaching the coast at Abbeville, thus sealing the trap for the First Army Group and the BEF. Three of the soldiers are armed with M98 rifles and are wearing the basic kit of a German soldier, including the M1935 steel helmet, gas-mask canister, ammunition box and entrenching tool. One of the soldiers is armed with an MP 38 submachine gun. The weapon was known by the soldiers as the Erma, and not the 'Schmeisser', as is popularly believed. The gun weighed 4.1kg (9lb) and fired a 32-round box magazine at a rate of 500 rounds per minute. Its muzzle velocity was 390m/s (1279ft/s).

ABOVE: More captured French and colonial troops being marched off to the rear and into captivity. Although their German captors treated most of the French soldiers humanely, colonial troops were not so lucky. When the colonial soldiers surrendered, they were sometimes humiliated and beaten by German soldiers for putting up a fanatical resistance. However, units of the *Waffen-SS* such as those of the *Totenkopf* (Death's Head) Division dealt with them more severely and usually took no prisoners, preferring to round up the North African troops and have them summarily shot on the spot.

ABOVE: A photograph showing colonial troops in a temporary PoW holding area which seems to have been set up in a field in northern France. These soldiers, consisting mainly of Algerians and Moroccans, have been issued with French uniforms. Most of these troops were badly trained and poorly equipped and did not stand a chance against their superior opponents. Many of the exhausted and hungry troops spent the rest of the war in labour camps, while others enlisted in the *Wehrmacht* and saw action on the Eastern Front, and in North Africa fighting alongside General Erwin Rommel's *Afrika Korps*.

ABOVE: A group of German troops have gathered inside a field overlooking a village not far from the Channel coast. Judging by the appearance of the buildings, they have certainly suffered from aerial bombardment at the hands of the *Luftwaffe*. The state of the destroyed houses suggests that Allied troops must have retreated through the village towards the coast and consequently have come under heavy attack. Many villages and towns, especially in the coastal area, were subjected to a series of heavy aerial bombardments.

BELOW: Captured French troops are marched off to the rear to end the war as PoWs. These soldiers had fought a futile, costly battle of attrition in the Arras sector against overwhelming enemy superiority. By 23 May 1940, the 11th Schützen Brigade, supported by heavy air attacks, surrounded the town of Arras and fought a heavy contact with BEF and French forces. A number of prisoners were captured, which forced the rest of the defenders, including the British 'Petreforce' in Arras, to withdraw behind the Bethune–La Bassée Canal.

ABOVE: German and French soldiers have been laid to rest in the same military graveyard in northern France. The Frenchman whose grave is shown in the centre of the photograph is a Sergeant Charles Chomont, whilst in the foreground is the grave of a German soldier named Ferdinand Weger. It was a common practice, especially for soldiers of the German Army, to bury the war dead and leave the soldier's steel helmet on top of the headstone as a mark of respect.

ABOVE: German soldiers from an unidentified regiment pay their respects to their war dead during a military funeral in northern France on 23 May 1940. Although casualties were much lighter in the West than first expected, these compulsory German military ceremonies held for their war dead were still unquestionably a very sombre affair for the soldiers that had to endure them. It was especially difficult for those men that had lost close comrades in the front lines.

LEFT: When there were many burials to be carried out, as in the photograph shown here, huge trenches were normally dug in order to bury the war dead. The corpses of the soldiers were then individually laid to rest, alongside each other, in a long 1.8 or 2.1m (6 or 7ft) deep trench. Earth was then use to cover the bodies before a cross was placed next to where each dead soldier had been laid. This type of burial was also common practice among other countries, for example for French and British troops. However, in the case of officers and other high-ranking soldiers, the dead were normally buried in individual graves.

ABOVE: A motorcycle unit, along with infantry mounted on bicycles which are probably attached to a motorized reconnaissance unit, are about to pass a lorry that has been unloaded of its supplies. The motorcyclists, all of whom are armed with Mauser rifles slung over their shoulder, have their supplies attached to the back of their bikes on panniers. Apart from the rolled-up *Zeltbahn*, they carried the basic kit of an infantry soldier and spares for their motorcycles. They are wearing the rubbersized waterproof motorcycle coat, which in 1940 was manufactured in dark blue/green.

RIGHT: Two officers in a command post make general checks and plans prior to the next phase of operations against the retreating BEF and French forces. The maps are sprawled out across a table, allowing the men to retain a perpetual eye on the unfolding events in northern France. A field telephone can be seen, a vital communication link between other command centres and the front lines. By this point commanders employed mass firepower and tanks to punch their way through the increasingly thinly held enemy defences.

ABOVE: An artillery regiment passes through a French village, watched by French and British prisoners. This photograph was taken south of Boulogne on 20 May 1940. The regiment may have been attached to the 2nd Panzer Division, which was given the task of driving to the outskirts of Boulogne and taking the town from the British commander, Brigadier William Fox-Pitt. Fox-Pitt had orders to defend the town to the last man and last round. While he organized a hurried defence in the hills surrounding the port, British troops, under a storm of heavy fire, were being evacuated from the port by British warships.

RIGHT: 19 May 1940 – a motorcycle combination passes the wreckage of battle. French and British vehicles have been moved off the road to prevent congestion. The carnage of burnt-out and destroyed vehicles lay on miles of roads through Belgium and France as, in a desperate attempt to reach the coast, Allied forces had destroyed unnecessary equipment. But they were almost defenceless against the panzers and *Luftwaffe:* the armoured might of Hitler's panzer divisions was lined up 80km (50 miles) from the Channel coast, preparing for the final assault.

ABOVE: Taken on 24 May 1940, this picture shows captured troops waiting to be transported to hastily erected PoW camps in the rear. It was on this day that Hitler issued his directive No.13 in which he made known his strategic intentions for the days ahead. 'The next object of our operations,' he said 'is to annihilate English, French and Belgian forces which are surrounded in Artois and Flanders, by a concentric attack by our northern flank and by the swift seizure of the Channel coast in this area. The task of the *Luftwaffe* will be to break all enemy resistance on the part of the surrounded forces, to prevent the escape of the English forces across the Channel and to protect the southern flank of *Heeresgruppe* [Army Group] A...'

RIGHT: More captured French colonial troops being marched away to the rear as PoWs. Almost 400,000 colonial soldiers made up the French Army in 1940. Although badly trained and equipped, they fought in southern France against Italian forces, and in the north of the country against some of the German Army's most superior elements. However, unlike French, Belgian or British prisoners, they were seen by their captors as second-class citizens, and were occasionally treated with brutality, and sometimes even executed.

ABOVE: A chance to see a 10.5cm (4.13in) 18 howitzer firing at enemy positions south of Boulogne on 23 May 1940. The gun weighed 1985kg (4376lb) in action and fired a 14.81kg (32.6lb) shell to a maximum range of 10,675m (11,674yd). It was developed in the 1920s and first appeared in 1935 as an effective weapon in the new German Army.

ABOVE: An unusual sight: a motorcyclist being towed after his vehicle has apparently developed a mechanical fault. The BMW R35 was normally a very reliable motorcycle and was used widely throughout the German Army in 1940. For the campaign in the West, a whole battalion of a panzer division's rifle brigade were given BMW R35s. On these motorcycles the soldiers rode into battle and dismounted to fight, just as dragoons in an earlier century had done with their horses.

ABOVE: In northern France, German troops hastily remove a truck from the road that was more than likely causing severe congestion. Abandoned or damaged trucks left behind by the Allies after Stuka attacks delayed both the Allied retreat and the German pursuit. Any vehicle that could not move under its own power would be ruthlessly pushed off the road to maintain the pace of the advance. The men wear the standard basic kit of a German soldier. Of particular interest in this picture are the rifle-ammunition pouches, as well as the normal pattern leather 'Y' straps of their webbing harness.

ABOVE: Soldiers belonging to the 7th Panzer Division come across an abandoned French Hotchkiss H-39 tank somewhere in northern France. As the retreat along the Channel coast gathered momentum, more and more Allied vehicles fell to the onrushing armoured spearheads of the *Wehrmacht*. General Erwin Rommel, commander of 7th Panzer Division, noted in his diary that once, when several French tanks were captured, he incorporated them into his own column still with their French drivers. 'Captured officers,' he noted, 'were more concerned about permission to keep their batmen.'

BELOW: A photograph taken by a soldier belonging to the 2nd Panzer Division, probably during its drive on Boulogne, as it is dated 22 May 1940. It appears that the horse-drawn cart has come under direct aerial attack, as the driver attempted to leave the open road in order to avoid the merciless rounds of bullets. Both the horses and the bullet-riddled French soldiers that frantically abandoned the cart lie in the field together. Scenes like this became more common during this period of the campaign as Herman Göring stepped up his *Luftwaffe* attacks along the coastline of the Channel.

ABOVE: The crew of a PzKpfw 35(t) are carrying out repairs to what appears to be the main armament of this Czech tank. With the take-over of Czechoslovakia in March 1939, the *Wehrmacht* consequently gained a number of valuable resources, and about one-third of the panzer strength available in May 1940 originated from Czech factories. Some 140 PzKpfw 35(t) served in the panzer divisions. The 't' stands for *Tchechoslowakisch* [Czechoslovak]. This photograph gives a good view of cupola that incorporated four episcopes and a one-piece circular hatch. The hull and turret are made of riveted plates.

ABOVE: A group of infantrymen with a captured French soldier holding a flagpole is being led away into captivity. It is of particular interest to note that as a humane concession, the Germans have allowed the soldier to retain the flag. The soldier at the front with his Mauser rifle on his shoulder is wearing a fur-covered pack. Even as late as 1940, some of the soldiers in the German Army were still seen wearing these old-style packs, complete with rolled-up blankets.

RIGHT: Two officers pose in front of a knocked-out PzKpfw 35(t). It appears to have received a direct hit and caught fire. The vehicle was armed with two 7.92mm (0.31in) machine guns that were belt-fed and air-cooled. Its main armament was an adaption of the Skoda A3 37mm (1.45in) antitank gun, fitted with a simple muzzle brake. The gun fired armour-piercing shot at a muzzle velocity of 675m/s (2215 ft/s) which was more than capable of penetrating 30mm (1.2in) of armour at about 549m (600yd). The tank was a very popular weapon with its crews during 1940, and was used widely by the members of the 6th Panzer Division.

LEFT: An antiquated Renault FT, dating back to World War I, of which there were 1500 still serviceable, being inspected by two German soldiers. This vehicle has probably run out of fuel and was abandoned by its crew. Although the Renault FT was a match for the PzKpfw I, its firepower and lack of manoeuvreability against larger panzers made it vulnerable. Unlike the Germans, the Allies placed less reliance on armour and aircraft, and even antitank and antiaircraft weapons. Whilst the French and British used outdated tactics, their opponents practised the theory of *Blitzkrieg*.

ABOVE: A Hotchkiss H-39 tank, after attempting to escape across country, has been knocked out of action. The Hotchkiss mounted an old-fashioned 37mm (1.45in) gun, but this was a low-velocity weapon which was fairly ineffective against the German panzers. Certain other factors contributed to the ineffectiveness of the French tank and its deployment against enemy armour. The majority of French tanks in operation were lacking in radio equipment and, perhaps more importantly, their crew's training was inferior and they were used only in small numbers rather than concentrated into a large unit.

ABOVE: Civilians trudge through a town in an attempt to escape the German armoured onslaught. Thousands of civilians were driven from their homes across the Low Countries and northern France as the Germans advanced. Either bombed out, or frightened at the prospect of falling into enemy hands, many collected their belongings and headed west or south. With so many refugees on the move, many main roads became severely congested, which not only hindered the attackers, but also made the Belgian, French and BEF troops' defensive deployment and withdrawal more difficult to implement.

BELOW: Destroyed British vehicles lay sprawled for miles on the beaches of Dunkirk following the evacuation of the BEF in late May and early June 1940. As disaster loomed in France for the entire Anglo-French armies, it had become clear to the British that their hopes would rest entirely on evacuating Dunkirk and its beaches. For a number of days, thousands of exhausted, dishevelled troops with a large assortment of vehicles – ranging from armoured cars to ambulances – swarmed through Dunkirk and on to the beach. These vehicles were almost definitely destroyed by the constant attacks of the *Luftwaffe*.

BELOW: Just outside Dunkirk, a group of captured French soldiers are being led away following days of bitter fighting in the town, watched by a smiling motorcycle reconnaissance. Relations between the French and the British had become seriously strained during the evacuation of troops from Dunkirk. The British were more concerned about a safe and effective evacuation for their troops, while the French regarded the port as a fortress, a base from which the Allies could launch the counterattack that would somehow undermine the German thrust then taking place across France.

LEFT: A soldier holding the rank of *Spiess* (RSM or 1st Sergeant) and wearing the M1936 German Army service tunic is reporting to his commanding officer inside the wreckage-strewn town of Dunkirk following its successful capture. It had been along this road that a swirling mass of despondent men, taking their horses and guns with them, clogged the streets leading down to the beach. Thousands of French, British, and Belgian soldiers crammed into the dwindling perimeter in and around the town, hoping that an evacuation from the sea would arrive to save them at any possible moment.

ABOVE: A British grave stands as a grim reminder of the suffering on the beaches of Dunkirk. As the ships came in to take the troops off the beach, those that were left behind waited in vain. Some soldiers suffered terribly from the fury of the *Luftwaffe*. With little to defend themselves except rifles and Bren guns, the soldiers were fully exposed. To escape the falling bombs, some men dug deep foxholes on the beaches. Others took strange measures to avoid being killed. During air raids, some were seen lying face down for more than an hour, hoping that enemy aircraft might think them dead.

ABOVE: Destroyed boats at Dunkirk in early June 1940 following the capture of the town and port. Air activity had been so fierce that in the burning harbour two French ships, a freighter and a transport, were hit and sunk by Ju87 Stuka dive-bombers. At night, the Germans lit up the sky with flares in order to continue shelling and bombing the beach and the port.

ABOVE: More ships sunk in the port of Dunkirk show to what extent the Luftwaffe went to attack everything that floated. In early June 1940, the pace of evacuation rapidly accelerated as a multitude of boats in all shapes and sizes went in, one after another, weaving between the wrecks in the water and returning heavily laden with men. On larger ships, jammed tight with men, it was common practice to leave watertight doors open to increase capacity, but the top-heavy vessels rolled over. Soon the water was bobbing with the dead, and through these floating corpses, the living swam for their lives. In total there were some 240 boats sunk, but over 330,000 men – including one-third of the French Army – were rescued by sea. However, the so-called 'Miracle of Dunkirk' partly came about thanks to Hitler's order to halt his armies from destroying the pocket.

ABOVE: One of many ships that failed to escape back across the turbulent Channel waters to the southern coast of England. Judging by the extent of the damage, the vessel has received a number of direct hits, probably from a Ju87 Stuka. For nearly two weeks, every vessel that could cross the English Channel fearlessly sailed into Dunkirk, braving some of the most appalling conditions in order to rescue the Allied soldiers who were marooned on the beaches. From the ships that managed to evade being sunk, the crews were able to witness for themselves the dreadful reality of defeat.

CHAPTER FIVE

The End Comes

The Fall of France

Despite the capture of Dunkirk and other Channel ports, there was much fighting left to come in France. German forces still had to battle their way south, but the end was already inevitable for the remnants of the French Army. By this stage of the war, 61 French divisions had been destroyed, with only 49 divisions left with which to confront the new enemy onslaught.

LEFT: 6 June 1940 – a motorcyclist watches horse-drawn transport move into the Dunkirk perimeter following the successful capture of the town after the Allied evacuation.
FAR LEFT: A photograph of *Generalfeldmarschall* Hermann Göring in Paris, taking the salute inside his Mercedes car. It was a proud moment for the *Luftwaffe*, one which Göring cherished until his death six years later.

With the first phase of the battle completed, the second part of the war in the West began. This operation, codenamed Operation 'Red', also known as the 'Battle of France', opened on 5 June 1940. Operation 'Red' began with the divisions of the panzer group attacking along the whole line with a number of successful penetrating strikes. Then, on 10 June, Rundstedt's Army Group A was given the task of advancing southwards in the direction of the Rhône valley and the Alps, cutting off the French armies to the east, while Army Group C was to plunge its forces forwards and destroy what was left of the enemy. It was here, in north-eastern France, that the Germans were ordered to ensure the ultimate collapse of the Maginot Line, and prevent the attempted withdrawal of enemy forces towards the south-west. German forces were also to prevent the enemy from withdrawing from the Paris area, and those deploying themselves on the lower Seine were to establish a new front.

PARIS AND BEYOND

During the early evening of 14 June 1940, the first German troops, men of the 9th Infantry Division, entered Paris. Within an hour, the centre of the city had been reached. On their arrival, German soldiers had found the city empty. Only 700,000 of the five million of the city's inhabitants had remained. The rest had taken to the roads south of the city, trying frantically in vain to escape the clutches of the German onslaught. The French Government, however, had earlier moved from Paris to the city of Tours. Now it moved once again, to Bordeaux.

South of Paris, out on the battlefield, the French Army was dying a lingering death, despite its courage. It was under strength and, coupled with the lack of supplies and the virtual collapse of the communication system, was an army unable to sustain the war effort any longer. German air superiority and close cooperation with ground troops, along with deep penetration of mechanized units, had led to continued successes on all fronts.

For the rapid thrust south, the German High Command set two panzer groups – von Kleist's and Guderian's – side by side, and sent them thundering south on both sides of the Reims. These two powerful panzer groups caused a massive blow to the retreating enemy formations. By 15 June, advanced elements of the Guderain Group reported having successfully reached Bar-sur-Aube and Gray-sur-Saône, while armour of the von Kleist Group had driven its panzers into Saint-Florentin and Tonnerre. Two days later, the right wing of Guderian's XXXIX Army Corps reached the Swiss border. Its arrival caused elation among the men and its commanders. Guderian was so delighted by its success, he set off personally to congratulate his brave troops for their speed and great achievements.

With the arrival of German forces on the Swiss border a ring was thus closed around the remaining French troops who were now frantically withdrawing from Lorraine and Alsace. Guderain was able to move north-east and penetrate the Maginot fortifications from the rear using his powerful panzer group. This massive, impenetrable fortification, which stretched from the Swiss border at Basle to Luxembourg and was armed with some 200,000 French soldiers, was virtually useless against an attack from the rear. Despite determined resistance from the French, the Maginot Line, with its large array of heavily constructed bunkers and well-armed fortifications, was soon overrun and captured after bitter fighting.

The geography of France, with its lack of natural obstacles and converging valleys, made it the ideal country for an invader to attack, especially with armoured divisions. The German drive into France had been bold. It had reaped success against an army that was unable to grasp the true concept of modern warfare: *Blitzkrieg*.

In the days prior to the final capitulation of the French Army, the Germans continued their advance, fragmenting the trapped enemy until they were reduced to pockets of some 30,000 men, each of them required to surrender or face total annihilation. Motorized columns tore through streets, some already ravaged by battle. Everywhere, tanks chewed through enemy positions. The unparalleled drive had completely destroyed any chances the French had of re-assembling. Total confusion swept the French lines, and immobility was producing dire consequences. In most places, French soldiers were slaughtered, trapped or simply overrun. Soldiers escaping the massacre withdrew southwards while the Germans continued to follow them.

By this time it was estimated that some 500,000 soldiers had been captured. Large amounts of weapons and war materiel had fallen into German hands. To further demoralize the French, on 20 June the Italian Army, with some 32 divisions, had launched a series of attacks in the south against 6 French divisions, after a declaration of war on the French made days earlier. However, against a 185,000-strong army, commanded by General Olry, the Italians made little progress. They were no match for the well-trained and disciplined French Army of the Alps.

While the Germans fought the last remaining pockets of resistance, a buoyant Hitler, together with some of his headquarters staff, motored to the same woods near Compiègne where, in 1918, the Kaiser's representative had surrendered. It was here that the French delegation, led by General Huntziger, would sign an armistice treaty with Germany. The armistice took place inside the famous railway dining car, which had been hastily removed from a museum and transported back to its original site. The main German demands were to prevent further hostilities and to give the Reich security for further conduct of war against England. Hitler also made it clear he would not take over the French war fleet for his own use, but stipulated that France fund the German Army's occupation.

At first the French delegation refused to agree to the terms. For a few hours its members held their nerve and stubbornly requested to transmit the terms to the French Government in Bordeaux. But by early evening, after spending nearly three hours in the railway dining car, the Germans lost their patience and gave the French a final ultimatum: to sign the armistice, or face further bloodshed out on the battlefield. Finally, at 18.50 hours, after more telephone conversations with Bordeaux, General Huntziger signed the armistice treaty and, by doing so, sealed France's fate.

TOTAL DEFEAT

By 25 June 1940, some German spearheads had advanced as far as Lyon. Panzers were reported to be outside Bordeaux, and even inside Vichy. But when the armistice took effect, German forces immediately withdrew. The *Wehrmacht* astonished by the speed and technical ingenuity of the victory against the West, behaved well against its defeated and dejected foe.

The French Army, however, was totally demoralized, literally shell-shocked, at the catastrophe that had befallen it. Some 94,000 French soldiers had been killed and about a quarter of a million had been wounded. Almost two million French soldiers were taken prisoner by the Germans. By contrast, the German losses were much less, with 27,000 dead and 111,000 wounded.

Rommel had called the attack 'A lightning *Tour de France*'. Virtually nothing remained of the French Army. Infantry, cavalry and armoured divisions were leaderless, directionless, and exhausted, as well as starving. Columns of dejected troops filed for miles along congested, war-torn roads that had been blackened by the smoke of battle. Among these men were young conscripts, older recruits, Poles and Czech volunteers, Arab light infantrymen, black Senegalese: all were the last remnants of an army that had tried to stem the colossal tide of *Blitzkrieg*, but had been swamped by it.

The battle of France had ended successfully for the Germans, and they reaped the fruits of yet another dramatic *Blitzkrieg* campaign. France had provided the perfect terrain for undertaking such a lightning war, and its conception seemed flawless. Yet untenable mountains, endless Russian steppes, and vast, empty deserts would from now on seriously hamper the practice of using *Blitzkrieg* to attain a fast and devastating victory against a stunned enemy.

RIGHT: German soldiers examine an abandoned British Vickers Mk VI light tank inside a forest in northern France. Much of the discarded armour found during this period in late May/early June 1940 had been destroyed by the withdrawing Allied troops. This Mk VI light tank, however, appears to be intact, which perhaps indicates that the crew had run out of fuel and did not have time to set fire to it.

ABOVE: The same British Vickers Mk VI light tank somewhere in northern France, probably a short distance from the Channel coast. These British light tanks proved to be of little use when faced with better-armed and armoured German vehicles. In 1940, the Mk VI served primarily as a command and reconnaissance vehicle. Like the French, the British had designed tanks mainly to support infantry formations, rather than use them as an offensive force in their own right.

BELOW: A soldier examines a captured British Bren carrier that belonged to the 4th/7th Royal Dragoon guards near Arras in late May 1940. As they did with the French Renault/AMX UE tractor, the German Army also pressed these Bren carriers into service in 1940, and their new owner widely utilized them until the end of the campaign. They had excellent cross-country capabilities and were able to carry a load of up to 500kg (1102lb) in the cargo compartment.

ABOVE: An interesting photograph showing the commander of 7th Panzer Division, General Erwin Rommel, on a field telephone in France in late May 1940. He is more than likely up with the leading elements of 25th Panzer Regiment as the photograph was taken near the La Bassée Canal in the area of **Cuinchy** on 27 May. Rommel's rapid advance had taken his panzer division through the wooded terrain of the Ardennes with its many narrow defiles and steep hills. On 16 May, once his armoured units had moved across into France and headed northwards, the route was canalized by woods or villages, but there was little to impede deployment or rapid cross-country movement. During his furious advance, a large number of French vehicles, including tanks, were overrun without opposition. These tanks were then ordered to accompany the German column, while unarmoured vehicles and dismounted men were ordered to march eastwards into captivity.

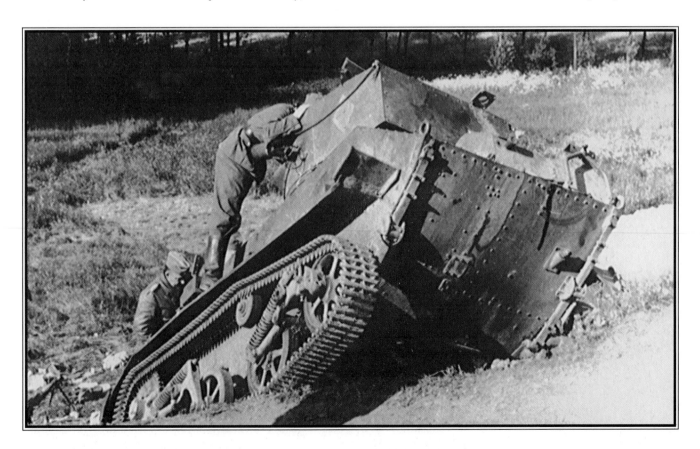

ABOVE: A knocked-out Vickers Mark VI light tank, this one probably belonging to the 9th Queen's Royal Lancers of the 1st Armoured Division, as this was photographed between Saint-Maxent and Huppy in late May 1940. The *Wehrmacht* report for 28 May records that on that day on the Somme, 30 enemy tanks had been destroyed, 9 of them by a German 3.7cm (1.45in) PaK gun that was attached to the 14th Company of 25th Infantry Division, of 2nd Infantry Division (motorized).

BELOW: A soldier trudges through the rain past German war graves, a number of stark and simple white crosses, at the edge of a forest in late May 1940. The infantryman can distinctly be seen wearing his *Zeltbahn*, an item of the German Army equipment which was designed and issued to be used as a waterproof cape. There were a number of ways of wearing it for marching, riding a bicycle and horse-riding. A number of *Zeltbahnen* could be joined together to form a four-man 'pup' tent. When not in use, it was always folded or rolled, before being strapped on to field equipment.

BELOW: French civilians work to clear the wreckage of their homes in Dunkirk. Judging by the extent of the damage, the *Luftwaffe* made sure that any resistance by the Allies was quickly neutralized by heavy, sustained low-level dive-bombing attacks. Hundreds of soldiers had been killed in Dunkirk as a result, as well as a substantial amount of civilians.

BELOW: This picture shows the extent of damage around the church in Dunkirk after the town was captured. Almost immediately after the town fell into German hands, captured French troops – together with gangs of civilians – were pressed into clearing the rubble. On the beach, too, there was a huge clearing operation to remove the many hundreds of burnt-out vehicles that were strewn for miles across the cratered sand. However, this clearing operation was not implemented until official German photographers had taken a series of photographs to be used for propaganda purposes back home.

BELOW: *Generalfeldmarschall* Hermann Göring donned in his familiar new-style white summer tunic during his visit to Paris. Despite Göring's failed attempt to use the *Luftwaffe* to destroy the BEF on the beaches of Dunkirk, three weeks later he was able to revel in the glory of victory over a defeated France. As Commander-in-Chief of the *Luftwaffe*, he had personally taken control of the air force in the West, and it had used its *Blitzkrieg* tactics with brutal effect. Throughout the campaign, Göring's faith in his men and the machines they flew was vindicated. Virtually all of Europe was now in the Germans' grasp, and Göring felt, perhaps with justification, that his air force had played the major part in the success.

BELOW: German soldiers marching through the centre of Paris on 14 June 1940. These men of the 9th Infantry Division were the first German troops to enter the French capital. The main ceremonial entry was made later in the day by elements of the 8th Infantry Division, who marched past the Arc de Triomphe, under which a huge swastika flag had been hung.

LEFT: Infantry on horseback ride through the Porte de la Villete into Paris on 16 June 1940. These troops, more than likely belonging to the 30th Infantry Division, are joining the victory procession held two days after the first German troops entered the city. Along the Avenue Foch between the Arc de Triomphe and the Porte Dauphine, mounted officers and the one-armed divisional commander *Generalleutnant* (Major-General) Kurt von Briesen took the saluting base. While French citizens stood silently by, columns of German infantry and marching bands processed through the city, much to the Parisians' dismay.

BELOW: Although the ceremonial entry into Paris was made by elements of the 8th Infantry and 28th Infantry Division during the afternoon of 14 June 1940, two days later, the Germans held their victory parade in the capital, this time made by the 30th Infantry Division. In this photograph a military band plays while infantry march flawlessly past down near the Place de la Concord. The saluting base was located in the Avenue Foch, midway between the Arc de Triomphe and the Porte Dauphine.

ABOVE: Soldiers from the 8th Infantry Division rest in front of a Parisian café in late June 1940. Their Mauser rifles and personal kit is sprawled out in front of them. All over the city the German military dominated the scene. Already strategic locations like the railway stations had been sealed off and occupied. Troops had taken up defensive positions, and the foot of the Arc de Triomphe was well guarded. It would not be until after Hitler's visit to Paris in July 1940 that certain military security restraints were lifted, and Parisians were able to get back to some kind of normality.

ABOVE: In the suburbs of Paris, German military control is evident. A group of French civilians look on as more German troops pour through into the capital. A medium Horch cross-country car is parked by the roadside, and two infantrymen armed with Mauser rifles also watch the spectacle. These two soldiers are more than likely guarding a strategic position or a road which leads into the city.

BELOW: This photograph was probably taken after the victory parade on 16 June 1940, as a roadblock has been erected down the Avenue Foch. Security in the central district of Paris was heavy, and checkpoints were to remain a common feature until the very end of German occupation of the city. During the summer of 1940, only military personnel or those holding special passes or papers were allowed through this checkpoint.

ABOVE: The victory parade along the Avenue Foch on 16 June 1940. Two Horch vehicles from the 30th Infantry Division are about to pass the saluting base. The vehicle on the right is armed with an MG 34 machine gun with the lightweight Dreifuss 34 antiaircraft mount and a 50-round Gurttrommel 34 'basket' magazine and ring sight. The MG 34 was 122cm (48in) long and weighed 31.07kg (68.5lb) on the Dreifuss AA mount. With a muzzle velocity of 755m/s (2477ft/s), it had a maximum range of 2000m (2187yd) and fired at a rate of 800–900 rounds per minute. It was a very effective weapon and on its sustained mount in an AA role was more than capable of damaging, or even bringing down, an aircraft.

BELOW: A photograph belonging to a soldier of the 25th Panzer Regiment of Rommel's 7th Panzer Division. Artillery fire can be seen in the distance hitting enemy defensive positions or 'hedgehogs' near a French village. The Allied forces in France were now deployed along the front in a series of 'hedgehogs', small defensible positions dug in along forests and villages, rather than in one continuous front. Various arms defended these 'hedgehogs', including antitank, antiaircraft gunners, infantrymen and artillerymen. The Allies were determined to defend these positions, and some were given orders not to retreat, but to hold out as strongpoints, even as German troops passed by them, in an attempt to disrupt the enemy's advance.

ABOVE: A *Wehrmacht* general greets Western Front commanders in June 1940. Like the tunics worn by officers, the service tunic worn by generals and ranks above was of very good quality material and usually of much higher degree of finish than the standard tunics. Rank insignia was worn, red and gold collar-patches set against a dark blue-green collar-patches. Trousers or riding breeches could be worn with the service jacket, although most generals preferred to wear breeches. This particular general has been awarded with the Knights Cross, 2nd Class and has it proudly pinned to his left breast.

ABOVE: Three officers from the 25th Panzer Regiment of 7th Panzer Division in a field overlooking enemy positions. The officer on the left wears the grey-green leather greatcoat and officer's riding boots with spurs. The picture is dated 11 June 1940; during this period the 7th Panzer Division attacked the port of St Valéry-en-Caux. Reports said that this was another Dunkirk but this time Rommel was determined to take prisoners. On 12 June, the 7th Panzer Division captured 40,000 prisoners, of which 8000 were British, including General Fortune, commander of the 51st Highland Division.

ABOVE: Sitting on a sidecar combination, an officer from the widely dispersed 25th Panzer Regiment poses for the camera with his men on 14 June 1940, south of St Valéry-en-Caux. By this time, reports confirmed that German troops had begun to cross the Seine without difficulty or opposition. Infantry divisions were now marching south towards the Loire. On 17 June the 7th Panzer Division, still exhilarated by the success at St Valéry, was ordered across the Seine. The unit was to drive west as fast as possible before swinging north in order to capture the strategic port of Cherbourg.

RIGHT: A colonial soldier belonging to a French African division has surrendered, and is taking a drink from a tin cup. Behind him stand several badly depleted and exhausted troops who have been gathered together as the remnants of a multitude of smashed units. These soldiers were captured by troops of the 7th Panzer Division who had withdrawn across France while trying to avoid the impending German armoured spearheads. By the time the sun had gone down on 18 June 1940, Rommel's armour and artillery were in position and covering the approaches to Cherbourg, ready to launch their attack against the port.

RIGHT: Colonial troops captured by soldiers of the 7th Panzer Division. Both these African men are wearing French greatcoats and French steel helmets. Some of these captured soldiers would be offered the chance to enlist to fight in North Africa with Rommel's *Afrika Korps*. Although these men had fought with courage in the face of overwhelming odds, they were so badly trained and under-equipped that they could do nothing else than temporarily hinder the German advance. A year later, in the deserts of North Africa, these troops would experience the same problem, this time fighting against the British.

ABOVE: Captured Allied prisoners of war march eastward in a column following their capture by the 7th Panzer Division. Most of them are still kitted with greatcoat, blanket with haversack, and a rolled groundsheet. The coat or blanket would be used as a cover for sleeping. Many of these troops, however, had not had much time for sleep before their capture, being kept constantly on the march, or fighting in 'hedgehog' positions against a storm of lethal German weaponry.

ABOVE: More French troops being marched off to a hastily erected PoW camp in the rear. The majority of soldiers are still kitted out with greatcoat, blanket with a haversack, and a rolled groundsheet. These men were captured by troops of Manstein's corps which had defeated the last coordinated Allied armoured attack of the campaign north of Le Mans. Dwindling in numbers, low in morale and totally unsupported by air, the soldiers were unable to repel a German counterattack and were easily defeated. By 22 June 1940, Manstein's force was across the Loire and victoriously forging ahead, with no resistance.

LEFT: A German field kitchen is set up on a riverbank while the crew watch vehicles making their way across a nearby bridge built by the engineers they are waiting to feed. The engineers have constructed a makeshift river crossing, resourcefully utilizing felled trees coupled with standard bridge-building equipment. In service with bridge-building units was a miscellany of equipment that usually consisted of pontoons, submerged barges, and various rafts, suitable for bridging most rivers or canals. Bridging platforms that were suitable for carrying loads of between 4.5 and 16 tonnes (5 and 14.5 tons) in weight would also be carried.

LEFT: A soldier on foot leading his horse trudges through a devastated French town that appears to have been subjected to heavy *Luftwaffe* attacks. Bombing raids like these on residential areas were purely aimed at military targets. This unknown town may have been of military value to the French or its forces had put up some kind of resistance against a German assault on the town. The method of *Blitzkrieg* was to bypass and avoid large opposition, infiltrate where possible, and fight only when there was no alternative. The momentum of attack was vital and in order to keep it going, air support was widely used.

LEFT: Destroyed buildings surround the church in the town of Dunkirk which stands as a grim reminder of the cost to France and Britain of the campaign in the West. In some areas, the fighting inside the Dunkirk perimeter had been fierce and the Germans found resistance particularly strong. The attack through the town was carried out by the 1st Panzer Division. Hitler's bodyguard, the *Leibstandarte*, were attached, and lost a number of men to the British Gloucestershire Regiment. Once victory had been attained, soldiers of the 1st Panzer Division hoisted a German national flag from the church tower.

ABOVE: German officers standing next to a Horch medium cross-country car discuss the next strategic move in France east of Belfort on 18 June 1940. It was on this day that XXXXI Corps captured the town of Belfort following a brief engagement between corps artillery and the fortified towers and citadel of the town. By the following day, the town was completely encircled and units of the First Army sealed the last exit for the Allies from north of the pocket. Some 200,000 men from the French Third, Fifth and Eighth armies were now trapped, and would remain so until the armistice and the end of the fighting.

ABOVE: Abandoned French artillery near Belfort on 19 June 1940. The field gun is a 155mm (6.1in) C Modele 1917. Horse-drawn carts, together with dead horses and smashed and burnt-out vehicles, lie nearby as a grim reminder of the superiority of the German land and air forces. The battle of France was now virtually over. Despite the collapse of the French Army, some French units fought on courageously.

RIGHT: A crew member of a 15cm (5.9in) heavy gun howitzer team has laid one of his shells out on a wicker mat to the side of the firing position. Wicker shipping containers with shells are stocked together, ready to be primed for firing. These shells could be hurled to an effective maximum range of 13,250m (14,500yd). Wicker containers were a cheap and effective means of storing shells safely, and they were often recycled.

ABOVE: The crew of a 3.7cm (1.45in) Pak 35/36 antitank gun is being wheeled into position in an attempt to neutralize the last remaining pockets of resistance inside a French town. Three soil-filled boxes of ammunition have been attached to the front of the gun's shield to counter weight on the front, and also to afford added armoured protection. To their left, a dismounted cyclist with the rank of private looks down on his dead comrade, who lies face down, still clutching his Mauser rifle.

RIGHT: An excellent photograph showing clearly the breech area of a German sFH 18 heavy gun and giving a good indication of its size. Once the breech of the gun was opened, the 43.52kg (96lb) projectile would be loaded forcefully into the barrel using a long rammer. Then followed the cartridge case with the specified number of charges. While this was being undertaken, some quick and final adjustments were made, with the gun-layer once again checking the base-line direction for firing. With the elevation set, the shell would then be ready to be fired. Of special interest is the gunner on the left, holding a notepad in his hand; he is more than likely the platoon commander.

138

BELOW: A sFH 18 heavy gun set up in a field overlooking scattered enemy positions. Lots of foliage has been applied around the gun to conceal it from the preying eye of the enemy. Although this photograph was taken on 19 June 1940, by which date the battle of France was almost at an end, gun crews were determined not to take any chances and so applied camouflage extremely carefully. The non-elevated barrel suggests that this gun is not in its firing position.

ABOVE: A long column of vehicles have come to a halt on a congested road north of Paris. A sFH 18 heavy gun is being towed on a gun carriage. The letter 'B' painted in white on the rear of the gun more than likely indicates that it is the second gun in the battery. The Opel Blitz truck behind the gun, which appears to have radio equipment stored on board, has the German national flag spread out across its roof in order to prevent it being attacked by the *Luftwaffe*.

LEFT: A French civilian trudges past a moving sFH 18 heavy gun which is being towed by a SdKfz 7 half-track. The sFH 18 gun proved its worth during the battle of France, despite the speed of its advance compared to the armoured spearheads. The weight of these artillery pieces and the way in which they had to be towed and positioned in the field proved that more tracked vehicles were needed. The German Army provided its divisions with half-tracks in the 1930s. These ranged from the 4.5 tonne (5 ton) *Leichter Zugkraftwagen*, or light prime mover, used to tow antitank guns and light antiaircraft guns, through to the 7.5cm (2.95in) to 15cm (5.9in) guns and pontoon bridge sections, to the huge 16.3 tonne (18 ton) *Schwerer Zugkraftwagen*, or heavy prime mover.

ABOVE: An interesting photograph showing captured French troops on a riverbank watching their captors as they ferry a 3.7cm (1.45in) PaK 35/36 antitank gun across to the bank. Jerrycans have been used to counterweight the gun, attached to the sloping splinter shield. Although the gun only weighed 432kg (952.5lb), moving it was sometimes a laborious task requiring the full strength of the crew. The process of equipping infantry divisions with guns was varied and changed numerous times during the course of the war. In 1940 the antitank gun proved itself on the Western Front, especially for its mobility and firepower, where it could advance alongside attacking infantry. But all antitank guns, especially the PaK 35/36, were of limited use as infantry support weapons.

ABOVE: The soldier on the right of this picture is talking to a member of the medical branch of the *Wehrmacht*. He is wearing a bright red cross on a plain white band that was always worn on the left upper arm. Medical personnel also included drivers of medical units. In 1940, the recovery of wounded men in the field by these medical units was normally fast and effective. Hospitalization or tending to injured soldiers at the front was all part of a medic's job. With some 160,000 men injured during the campaign, German medical personnel were kept very busy. However, it would not be until the war on the Eastern Front during the harsh winter of 1941 that these medics would find themselves overstretched.

ABOVE: A column of horse-drawn artillery advances across the rolling countryside in northern France. An ever-adaptable *Zeltbahn* has been placed over what appears to be a 10.5cm (4.1in) leFH 18 light field howitzer. This 10.5cm gun, developed by Rheinmetall, entered service in 1935 and was the standard field piece of the light batteries of the German Army. It weighed 1985kg (4377Ib) and fired a 14.8kg (32.6lb) shell. Due to the lack of motorized transport available in 1940, a number of these guns were towed by horses instead of using the preferred method of moving them by half-track.

ABOVE: A PzKpfw I moves along a congested road with the rest of the column of supply trucks and horse-drawn transport towing artillery. Draped on the engine deck of the panzer is the swastika flag. As with a number of vehicles that saw operations in the West, these flags were primarily used for aerial recognition. Thousands of vehicles continued to cram the roads going west, which ultimately caused massive traffic jams, sometimes of up to 24km (15 miles) long. Although moving cross-country could offer panzers a quicker and safer route for their advance, it dramatically increased fuel consumption.

ABOVE: Several crew members of a PzKpfw 35(t) have a chance to exchange stories during a rest break. The tankmen are wearing the black panzer *Feldmütze* and the special black panzer uniform that was of the same design and colouring for all ranks of the *Panzerwaffe* (tank arm), apart from the rank insignia. The panzer uniform comprised of a short black double-breasted jacket worn with long black trousers. The uniform was used both as service dress, including field service, and as a dress uniform. Two of the panzer men can be seen wearing the distinctive grey-green coloured leather greatcoat.

RIGHT: Various vehicles in a field, purposely spread out in case of aerial attack. A Horch Kfz 15 heavy cross-country car is parked while its driver and a dispatch rider take in the summer air. The rider's BMW R35 is behind the Horch vehicle. Among the other armoured vehicles and personnel carriers are two PzKpfw III Ausf A tanks. Despite problems with its suspension, the PzKpfw III defeated all of its opponents in the *Blitzkrieg* campaigns during both 1939 and 1940. Its main armament was a 5cm (1.9in) KwK L/42 cannon, and its secondary weapons were two MG 34 machine guns.

ABOVE: In a field in northern France a multitude of vehicles have come to a halt. With no sign of combat in the area, soldiers and panzer crews can enjoy a little time to talk among themselves. PzKpfw 35(t), PzKpfw II, PzKpfw III and a Horch light staff car are purposely spread out across the column. On the right side of the staff car's mudguard is the panzer group command's command flag. All staff vehicles of German commands, as well as the personal or official vehicles of commanders, were authorized to display pennants or plates. For major army commands, like this one, the pennants were square plates, using black and pink pennants to denote the command of panzer units in a division.

146

CHAPTER SIX

Crises in the Desert

Arrival of the *Afrika Korps*

With the stunning achievements of *Blitzkrieg* in Europe, Mussolini, eager to share in Hitler's continuing military success, decided to invade Egypt from the colony of Libya in September 1940. His forces greatly outnumbered the British troops that were trying frantically to hold on to their meagre positions. Three months later, on 9 December, the British troops, commanded by General Sir Archibald Wavell, launched a limited counteroffensive against the Italian Army, which Marshal Rodolfo Graziani had led 97km (60 miles) inland across the baking-hot desert of Libya. In the five-day battle that ensued, the Italians were dealt a severe hammering by the Allied force, resulting in 38,000 Italians being captured for a total of only 624 British Commonwealth troops killed and wounded.

Other parts of the Italian Army were pursued deeper into Libya, and by early January 1941, an Australian force had besieged 45,000 Italian troops at the fortress of Bardia. By 5 January, these exhausted, depleted troops surrendered after the Italian commander, General Berganzoli, had left his men to their fate and fled for Tobruk. The British Commonwealth troops' commander, General Richard O'Connor, continued to push relentlessly through the desert, spearheading his force along the coast road to the lightly defended port town of Tobruk.

On 21 January, Tobruk fell, yielding another 27,000 prisoners from the Italian garrison. O'Connor's force, undeterred by exhaustion, carried on at breakneck speed, while remnants of the Italian invaders fell back on Tripoli, the capital of Libya. Along the coast road, the British 7th Armoured Division pursued the Italians relentlessly, until finally, on 7 February, the enemy surrendered at Beda Fomm. Mussolini had lost some 130,000 troops and 380

LEFT: Dozens of ships are anchored in the port of Tripoli following the first despatch of German troops, guns, armoured cars and tents to North Africa which took place on 14 February 1941.
FAR LEFT: Albrecht Kesselring, Rommel's commander-in-chief, visits a sector of the *Afrika Korps* front. Although an able commander in his own right, he was initially overshadowed by Rommel's success in the desert.

tanks in just two months. It was a major humiliation to the Italian dictator. He was now compelled either to ask for help from Hitler, or to face total disaster in North Africa.

ROMMEL SENT

Prior to the Italian invasion of Egypt, Hitler had offered Mussolini the assistance of a panzer division, but the Italian dictator, over-confident as ever, decided to decline the reasonable offer. Instead, Hitler watched the battle unfold, knowing that without his support the Italians would founder and be driven out of North Africa altogether. When Mussolini finally appealed for help, Hitler readily accepted, determined more than ever to restore Axis' prestige and consolidate the Reich's strategic position in North Africa.

Despite the defeat of the Italians, Hitler was very confident in victory. He was aware that the success of the British was not a result of their superiority, but due to the incompetence of Italian leadership. So it did not come as any great surprise that on 3 February 1941, Hitler chose one charismatic leader who would stamp his greatest achievements in the uncharted desert wilderness of North Africa, making him a living legend in his own right. His name was General Erwin Rommel, the great panzer leader who had steamrollered his 7th Panzer Division through France in 1940. Hitler realized that Rommel was probably the only general capable of leading an African force. Although Rommel's mission was ostensibly to explore the military situation, Hitler was quite aware, even at this early stage of war planning, that it would be the German troops fighting to prevent the British advance through Libya, and not the Italians.

On 12 February 1941, Rommel's Heinkel bomber had brought him to North African soil for the first time. The shimmering heat and inhospitable landscape did nothing to inspire this legendary commander. Nor did the fact that the Italians were still in full retreat towards Tripoli and eagerly packing their belongings to catch ships back to Italy before the British arrived. Two days after Rommel set foot in North Africa, thousands of tonnes of equipment, ranging from guns and armoured cars to tents and

BELOW: More ships inside the port of Tripoli. The first Germans to arrive in the port on 14 February 1941 comprised the advanced echelon troops of the 5th Light and 3rd Panzer Regiments, as well as reconnaissance soldiers and support units. Crossing the Mediterranean by sea was very hazardous for transport ships. In 1941 the British began waging an intense and relentless war against enemy transport ships and supplies travelling from Italy to Libya. Although the 5th Light and 3rd Panzer Regiments arrived unscathed, during the weeks and months to come, a number of transport ships would be attacked and sent to the bottom of the sea. At first, German supplies were transported on board German ships in the Mediterranean, but their losses had been so terrible that German troops and supplies were increasingly compelled to use Italian transports.

mosquito netting, were unloaded onto the floodlit dockside. Over the weeks that followed, more men and fresh supplies of equipment disembarked with the usual propaganda parade. To the waving spectators, there seemed no end to this military might, for Rommel had, in fact, cleverly ordered the tanks of the 5th Panzer Division to drive around the block to give the impression of a large army. Rommel was now determined to show the British, as he had done in France, of the great conquests he would win for Germany. In front of his commanders he told them that his first objective was the re-conquest of Cyrenaica, then, 'My second, northern Egypt and the Suez Canal.'

DRIVE EAST

In early March 1941, Rommel ordered General Johannes Streich's panzer force to drive eastwards along the coast from Syrte with advanced units of the 5th Light Division. By 4 March, Streich had confidently reached Mugtaa, and suddenly contacted enemy soldiers. Quickly and decisively they drove the British Army from its light defences with hardly a fight. There was nothing to stop Streich's men; they chased the enemy across the desert towards the little village of Mersa el Brega. Berlin's directive stipulated that Rommel was not to attack Mersa el Brega until the end of May. Rommel ordered its attack and, as predicted, the British abandoned their positions.

By early April the British, desperately trying to keep their forces intact, had begun a general withdrawal from the peninsula of Cyrenaica. Still unwilling as ever to allow the enemy time to regroup and bring up more armour, Rommel continued disobeying orders from Berlin and

instructed a dramatic, three-pronged assault, determined to exploit the enemy's confusion. Backed by two Italian divisions, German units attacked the British defenders and drove them back. In the aftermath that followed a trail of destruction led to the smouldering town of Benghazi. In a letter home to his wife Lucie, Rommel boasted about his one-man desert *Blitzkrieg*, but in Berlin, news of Rommel's exploits across the desert were met with consternation. Rommel was more convinced than ever of victory in North Africa and believed that the port of Tobruk was now within in his grasp.

RESISTANCE AT TOBRUK

Tobruk was the most important port in North Africa and since it was occupied by the British, Rommel's *Afrika Korps* dared not resume its offensive towards Egypt until the Tobruk garrison was eliminated. Unknown to Rommel, the British Prime Minister, Winston Churchill, had already ordered Tobruk 'to be held to the death without thought of retirement'. The British were determined that this was not going to be another Dunkirk. Tobruk would be remembered as the longest siege in British military history. On 11 April 1941, the *Afrika Korps* finally found out how strong the enemy garrison was. The fortress was held by the British Empire's toughest troops, who stubbornly replied to the German assaults with equally energetic bursts of gunfire. Rommel was so perplexed by the enemy's stiff resistance, and so angry, that he wired Berlin, demanding an airlift of the 15th Panzer Division.

ABOVE: Ships at harbour in the port of Tripoli following days of sailing across the turbulent and often hazardous waters of the Mediterranean. Over the months to come, the perilous crossing would cost the German Army dearly. Frequent attacks were made by the British. From the important island stronghold of Malta, British submarines and torpedo-carrying aircraft launched a series of deadly attacks on German convoys which were destined for Libya. In order to lessen the amount of troops being killed at sea, the men were flown by transport aircraft to Africa on an increasing scale. Moreover, dock installations at the port of Tripoli were limited and could not allow the unloading of more than three or four ships at a time. It was therefore an early imperative for the German forces to secure further ports along the coast and to defend its convoys with the aid of the Italian Air Force.

However, even when the first units of the 15th Panzer Division arrived days later, further attacks against the port failed miserably. The failure to pierce the British defences was to leave a festering thorn in Rommel's side. With a grudging acceptance, he now took the bold move of bypassing Tobruk, and proceeded to plunge the bulk of his *Afrika Korps* towards Sollum. By 14 June 1941, the Reich held its breath as a major enemy offensive at Sollum came face to face with Rommel's mighty *Afrika Korps*. The next day, under the scorching heat and choking dust clouds, a bloody and violent tank and infantry battle raged. Despite fighting against an uneven weight of armour,

Rommel's superior tactics, coupled with the stubborn resistance of the German and Italian troops, brought a much-needed victory.

ON THE RETREAT

Late on in the summer of 1941, the *Afrika Korps* was strengthened, upgraded and renamed *Panzergruppe Afrika* (Panzer Group Africa). It seemed invincible, now boasting six Italian divisions, and included the *Afrika Korps* – the 15th and 21st Panzer Divisions – and the 90th Light Division, which included old units of the 5th Light Division. At this point, troop strength numbered a total of 55,000 men. Ahead of the *Afrika Korps*, the British had also taken the opportunity to reinforce their army, and had reorganized the Western Desert Force as the British Eighth Army. It was from here on the Egyptian border that the British prepared to launch a massive offensive to destroy Rommel before he could knock out the Tobruk garrison. By November, the British reinforcements were assembled, with more than 100,000 troops and 700 tanks poised to attack in the baking sun.

On 18 November the eerie stillness of the desert was suddenly shattered as British guns began the offensive with a series of savage tank battles. Across an area of about 129km^2 (50 square miles) from the Egyptian frontier in the east to the road south out of Tobruk in the west, tanks duelled with tanks. Although the *Afrika Korps* was outnumbered, Rommel was determined to prevent the British from hammering a corridor through to Tobruk. In a stunning display of military tactics, he demonstrated his mastery of mobile operations against his British opponents and charged across the desert before linking up with German units at Halfaya Pass and Sidi Omar.

By late November, British lines had once again stiffened and, with further reinforcements, now began streaming towards Rommel's exhausted and overstretched lines. With no fuel, ammunition or reserves left, Rommel ordered a general retreat from Cyrenaica, including dismantling his siege apparatus east of Tobruk. For the first time in his life, he was on the retreat. On Christmas Day Benghazi fell into British hands and, by the end of 1941, Rommel was back to where he had begun that spring.

ABOVE: An Opel-Blitz truck is parked inside a camp outside Tripoli in late February 1941. Tents have been erected and a small makeshift field kitchen has been set up for the men to use. Between 14 and 20 February 1941, advance elements of the 5th Light Division had been arriving in Tripoli with thousands of tonnes of equipment and cars. This camp is just one of dozens which were erected to act as shelter and a base for the troops of the *Afrika Korps*. Although their stay in the camp would be very brief, many of the soldiers' first impressions of it (and the desert) were negative.

LEFT: Another camp, but this time erected near a temporary airfield near Tripoli. Soldiers that flew into Libya by Ju52 transporters quickly reached their new units. All reinforcements had to stay outside Tripoli, which was about 6.4km (4 miles) away. As the soldiers set up their makeshift camp, they could see barren terrain stretching far away into the distance. It was almost frighteningly primitive, and so hot, that many thought it almost impossible that a soldier could exist there. When not on duty, the troops would hide away in their tents as the scorching heat bore down on the dry, sandy terrain.

ABOVE: A soldier poses in front of his makeshift tent near Tripoli in late February 1941. The windscreen of the vehicle has been covered in order to make a useful sunshade. Conditions for the men were like nothing they had ever experienced before. Encamped in and around Tripoli, they were shocked by the land. A series of rolling sand dunes or flat, dry plains, a few cacti and palms, reminded some of the soldiers of a journey's end. Many men also wondered how heavy tanks would drive through the deep, sandy terrain, and wondered how they could survive the heat, for they had heard about the terrible debilitating effects of fighting in scorching terrain. The infantryman, unused to fighting in the high temperatures, thirsting across the arid wilderness, worried they might quickly dehydrate and die. If they were going to survive and beat the British, they would have to learn extraordinarily fast and improvise wherever, and whenever, they could.

BELOW: Taken from a Heinkel 111, this photograph shows more Heinkels on an airfield near Tripoli. Travelling by aircraft was the easiest and most effective way of supplying the troops and carrying out reconnaissance missions along enemy lines. By this period the Germans had already perfected the combined use of air- and ground forces in *Blitzkrieg* tactics. In the desert, the Heinkel, Junker Ju87 dive-bomber, Messerschmitt Me109s and Me110s conducted missions either to pinpoint enemy positions or to carry out ground-strafing roles. This particular Heinkel was more than likely carrying out a reconnaissance mission to pinpoint the enemy's location. In February 1941 German reconnaissance reports indicated that General O'Connor's Western Desert Force consisted of some 25,000 or so British and Commonwealth troops of 7th Armoured Division and 4th Indian Division, reinforced by the 6th Australian Division and New Zealand troops. Although these British and Commonwealth soldiers had succeeded in defeating the Italian 5th and 10th Armies, and were comprised of some 235,000 men, they were now going to face an entirely different calibre of troop and commander.

ABOVE: An Opel-Blitz field kitchen cross-country truck has come to a halt on a road. Its driver appears to have a jerry can ready to fill up the vehicle's empty tank. These four-gallon canisters not only carried fuel, but were also used to carry water, obviously a vital asset to soldiers who were stationed out in the desert. Because of the intense heat and the vast distances the vehicles had to travel, water was also used for the radiators of the motors. In fact, so essential was water for the *Afrika Korps* that when on the move through the African landscape, its men were accompanied by special water columns, each one equipped with portable water pumps. To save water, it was not uncommon for the men to wash with petrol.

ABOVE: An off-duty soldier makes sure he looks presentable by combing his hair with the aid of a shaving mirror. Most off-duty soldiers wore the bare minimum of clothing, usually shorts and shoes or boots. Living out in the desert and keeping clean was often difficult, especially if the camp was miles from the sea. For sake of hygiene, the men were issued with water basins that were made from impregnated canvas and could be folded together and put into a pocket. They had two field water bottles, which the soldiers regularly filled up with coffee. However, all water had to be boiled as the cisterns often contained leeches. Mosquitoes, too, were a problem for the *Afrika Korps*, due to the many dead salt lakes in the desert, compelling the men to put up mosquito nets each evening.

BELOW: An 8.8cm (3.45in) Flak 36 heavy antiaircraft gun is being prepared for deployment out in the desert. The gun was purposely designed for a dual-purpose role. The Flak 36 weighed 4985kg (10,992lb) and was mounted on a platform. It fired a 9.4kg (20.7lb) shell at a muzzle velocity of 795m/s (2609ft/s) (firing armour-piercing rounds against ground targets), and 820m/s (2691ft/s) (firing high-explosive rounds against aircraft). It could traverse 360 degrees and the gun could elevate from −3 to +85 degrees. It had a fire rate of 15 rounds per minute and a maximum vertical range of 8000m (8758yd). This 8.8cm gun was very effective against enemy armour and at a range of 2000m (2187yd) could penetrate 8.8cm (3.45in) and 7.2cm (2.8in) of vertical and 30-degree sloped armour.

ABOVE: Members of a *Luftwaffe* ground crew stand to attention next to their Messerschmitt Me109 during a visit by *Generalfeldmarschall* (Field Marshal) Kesselring, one of the most able of Germany's generals during World War II. In 1941 he was appointed Commander-in-Chief South, to share with General Erwin Rommel the direction of the North African campaign. Maintaining aircraft was a difficult task for ground crew in sandy conditions at temperatures of over 50 °C (122°F).

ABOVE: This photograph was taken by General Erwin Rommel himself, and shows a fast-moving column of panzers hurtling along a road near Mugtaa in May 1941. At times Rommel was seen clambering into his light Fieseler Storch plane to take personal control of his units' movements from the air. On occasion from his Storch aircraft he would fly at shoulder-height level and drop a message on a column: 'If you don't move off at once, I'll come down – Rommel!' To him speed was all that mattered. He hunted continuously for any column that had taken too long or had mistaken its direction. With his sudden presence and his sharp tongue, he goaded, improvised and galvanized every part of his command.

ABOVE: A soldier stands in front of a Horch cross-country car that has canvas sheeting protecting the front of the windscreen from sandstorms. His is wearing the *Deutsches Afrika Feldmütze* (cap) with aviator goggles. His shirt and trousers were issued to troops in North Africa and were very similar to the field-grey army shirt, but this garment was made of a hard-wearing cotton drill dyed to a darkish sand colour. As in this photograph, the shirtsleeves could be buttoned down or rolled up. The collar of the shirt was, in most circumstances, worn open at the neck.

ABOVE: Luftwaffe ground crew service a flying boat in Tripoli. As demand on the limited number of Junker Ju52s for supplying the *Afrika Korps* increased, large numbers of flying boats were pressed into service to bolster the level of supplies reaching Africa. There were a number of flying boats in use, making the difficult and perilous journey from Italy to North Africa. These aircraft types, especially the larger ones, were primarily used for supplying troops.

ABOVE: Soldiers have just had a swim in the Mediterranean at Benghazi, which fell on 4 April. They are getting dressed next to their Horch vehicle. Out in the desert, military regulations for uniform and hygiene were quickly ignored by the troops. Both the pith helmet, and later the khaki necktie, were discarded. Soon boots, either ankle or knee-high, were worn. The original tunics and breeches were soon to be exchanged for olive-green, lightweight cotton shirts and shorts gained from captured British supply depots. Their heavy greatcoats were not worn, but used as a cover during the freezing desert nights.

RIGHT: German soldiers have the chance to relax in the desert with their commanding officers next to a wall of sandbags. The barren landscape of the African desert stretches away behind them. Two of the men are using jerry cans as seating. Both men are wearing the *Deutsches Afrika Feldmütze*. A variety of military uniform styles existed within the ranks of the German Army personnel in North Africa. However, the bleaching effects of the combination of heat, sun and desert air on their uniforms made them look dirty, resulting in the alteration of the original colours and making them difficult to distinguish.

ABOVE: A British Mk VI Crusader I Cruiser tank has received a direct hit from German antitank fire whilst attempting to withdraw from Cyrenaica. This was one of the most distinctive of the British tanks, but because of its rushed design, it became one of the least effective on the battlefield. It was here in the Western Desert in June 1941 when it first saw combat that these problems became apparent. The Mk VI Crusader I Cruiser had a crew of five and its main armament was a two-pounder (40mm (1.57in) cannon. Its secondary armament was two 7.92mm (0.31in) Besa machine-guns (one co-axial in front turret). The tank weighed 19.3 tonnes (19 tons) and had a top road-speed of 43km/h (27mph) with a road range of 160km (100 miles).

RIGHT: German and British war graves next to a track remind passing soldiers of the cost of the fighting across the Western Desert. The battle had been a bloody contest of attrition. In Operation 'Crusader' alone, some 38,000 Germans were killed, wounded or missing. By May 1941, the *Afrika Korps* knew that the British were desperately trying to keep their forces intact. Rommel, however, unwilling as before to allow the British to re-group and bring up more armour, was determined to exploit the opportunity, despite the number of casualties this would inflict. What followed was a number of bloody tank battles.

RIGHT: A smiling soldier of the *Afrika Korps* inside his armoured car. The photograph was taken just after the *Afrika Korps* forces had managed to hold on to the Halfaya Pass. The attack on the Halfaya Pass was very effective, and Major Bach's men fought with great zeal. Although short of suitable weapons to use against the British Matilda tanks, they knocked out several, and the British withdrew, leaving 500 prisoners behind them. Of interest is the camouflaged tent or canopy on the back seat. When the vehicle was stationary and dug in for the night, the tent or canopy was attached to it for added protection against the harsh desert conditions.

ABOVE: General Kesselring with an Italian Air Force officer has just flown to North Africa in an Italian Savoia-Marchetti SM79-II. The value of disruptive camouflage on this aircraft can be seen in this photograph. The Savoia-Marchetti was one of the most important Italian bombers of World War II. It served widely in a normal bombing role, and was arguably one of the finest torpedo bombers of its time. It appeared in a number of theatres, including North Africa, the Balkans and the Mediterranean, while other units used them for large fast bombers in the anti-shipping role. This particular three-engined aircraft had 745.2kW (1000hp) Piaggio P.XI RC 40 engines. Its maximum speed was 434km/h (270mph) and it had an operational capacity of 11,300kg (24,192lb). Its main armament was a 12.7mm (0.5in) Breda-SAFAT gun set on the roof of the cockpit humpback to enable bullets to clear the nose propeller. Torpedoes could be hung externally from this aircraft.

BELOW: The back view of a Focke-Wulf Fw 189a-2 aircraft being serviced by the ground crew. This aircraft was a twin-boom tactical reconnaissance plane with extensively glazed nacelle. It was a very effective aircraft, manoeuvrable and sturdy. Its primary function was reconnaissance in North Africa, although later in the war it was used as a nightfighter. The plane had a crew of two and was powered by two 12-cylinder inverted-vee air-cooled 347kW (465hp) Argus AS 410A-1 engines. Maximum speed was 335km/h (181mph) with a range of 670km (362 miles). Armed with one 7.92mm (0.31in) MG 17 machine gun on the wing, and two 7.92mm MG 81 machine guns, it could carry four 50kg (22.68lb) bombs on the underwing racks.

ABOVE: A Dornier crew is just about to board its aircraft. The *Afrika Korps* were supported in many of their operations by the *Luftwaffe*. As a veteran of the successful *Blitzkrieg* war against the West in 1940, Rommel made clear not only the necessity of employing the *Luftwaffe* and its vital importance of air support with the ground forces, but also the necessity of air supply in desert conditions. The *Luftwaffe* was an essential component of *Blitzkrieg*. Rommel and Kesselring were both aware of the increasing Allied air superiority and knew that the enemy air force would be the deciding factor in all the battles to come.

ABOVE: A soldier poses in front of a downed British Curtiss Kittyhawk, the British equivalent of the P-40E Warhawk in service with the US Army Air Corps. With the closed cockpit hatch and extensive damage to the aircraft's exterior, it seems more than likely that the pilot did not survive the crash. The Kittyhawk superseded the Tomahawk, and was used largely in the fighter-bomber role. It did not compare well with the Messerschmitt 109 above low level, but at low level it was a better fighter than the Hawker Hurricane, the other major Allied fighter type in service at the time. It undoubtedly made a major contribution to the Allied war effort in North Africa. In contrast, particularly after the invasion of the Soviet Union in June 1941, the *Afrika Korps* never had as much support from the *Luftwaffe* as Rommel would have liked.

ABOVE: A group of senior *Luftwaffe* commanders around a table discuss plans for air support in North Africa. The commander sitting on the left wearing a white officer's *Schirmmütze* or uniform cap, is *Feldmarschall* Kesselring, Commander-in-Chief South, who also shared with Rommel the direction of the North African campaign. For operations in Africa, Kesselring had no inter-allied staff organized and had brought with him the staff of HQ Second Air Fleet. He had made it perfectly clear to them that the centre of gravity of the war against England lay in the Mediterranean. Already he had urged both Göring and Hitler to capture Malta, from where the British were continuing to cause serious problems to shipping supplying troops to North Africa. Sicily, Crete and the Aegean were also problem areas.

BELOW: A Fieseler Storch aircraft carrying *Feldmarschall* Kesselring leaves an airstrip for a short tour of the Western Desert. The Fieseler Fi56C Storch was probably one of the most popular aircraft used by the *Luftwaffe*, especially in the desert. Its main role was as a liaison aircraft; it was also used for reconnaissance. It was an extremely adaptable aircraft and was very important in the rapid advances and shifting front lines in the desert. It also had excellent STOL (short take off and landing) capabilities and provided perfect vision for the crew. This particular aircraft, as with most of the Storchs which saw service in North Africa, were finished in a sand-colour base. Of interest is the radio call sign letters on the side of the aircraft's tail, rather than the usual Staffel code.

ABOVE: *Feldmarschall* Kesselring, with two of his staff, visits *Luftwaffe* crews in the desert. Kesselring's visits were meant not only to oversee operations in North Africa, but also to instill courage and versatility in the men of the *Luftwaffe*. He was totally aware, as was Rommel, that the troops first had to get used to the extreme climate, terrain and vegetation. They had to quickly learn to adapt themselves to the combat tactics both of nature and of their new enemy. Once they had become acclimimatized, men and officers alike were equal to any task that the enemy might throw at them.

ABOVE: Wearing a life jacket, Rommel is about to fly back to Italy in a Heinkel 111. Rommel had absolute conviction in mobile operations and believed in leading his panzer force from the front, or as he said, 'from the saddle'. During operations out in the desert, Rommel was to be found again and again with the leading tank, the leading platoon or the leading company commander. At the head of a panzer column, he directed fire like a corporal, and with energy and enthusiasm, like some kind of mystic warrior, somehow encouraging his men, who were perhaps cowering under hostile fire, to move forwards and shoot. Being away from the front on trips to Italy and Germany made Rommel anxious. He worried that without his competent leadership, there would be a reversal of fortune in the desert.

ABOVE: The 'Desert Fox', *General der Panzertruppen* (General) Erwin Rommel confers with two of his staff on the next strategic move in the desert. Both the men are wearing greatcoats and carrying German Army issue torches. Rommel is wearing his famous looted British goggles, which he adored. He was not a very easy man to serve. Like so many German commanders, he could only command in his own way, learned in the trenches of World War I and then in France 22 years later. But the energy he generated on the battlefield printed an indelible image on the mind of every soldier in his command.

ABOVE: Two commanders take the salute before of their men prior to leaving for the front. The photograph must have been taken earlier in the campaign in North Africa, as the soldiers in the background are wearing German Army tropical sun helmets, or pith helmets, which were soon discarded as the campaign progressed. The helmets displayed two embossed metal helmet plates. On the right side, the shield bore the national tricolour of black, white and red, whereas the shield on the left showed a dull silver metal *Wehrmacht Adler* (eagle) raised from a black painted shield.

BELOW: A major makes some notes, resting on his leather folder. He wears a greatcoat and the best-known item of tropical field dress, the peaked field cap, or *Afrika Korps Feldmütze*. Made of dark olive material, which could vary towards either brown or green, it was lined inside with bright red material. Note the false flap on the side of the cap and the two ventilation eyelets. The machine woven eagle was dyed in pale blue-grey. The greatcoat he wears was a tropical version and was made in darkish brown woollen cloth. Unlike the continental version, it is double-breasted, with two rows of six painted buttons, and has a contrasting dark green face collar. His shoulder straps identify his particular rank of major.

ABOVE: Two Ju52 transports taxiing on a makeshift airstrip out in the desert. These aircraft were vital to the *Afrika Korps*, regularly shipping large quantities of supplies and troops from Italy to Libya and known affectionately as *Tante Ju* (Auntie Ju).

BELOW: Early April 1941 – Rommel's *Afrika Korps* drive out the British from Cyrenaica. From an artillery observation point, heavy gunfire can be seen pounding British positions. In the distance, past the smoke, enemy vehicles can just be seen withdrawing from the systematic bombardments. It was on 4 April 1941, under the shimmering high-noon sun, that Rommel's mixed force began their three-pronged assault into the raw desert of Cyrenaica. Along this trail – known as 'the path of death' to soldiers – this force would lead onwards to the Egyptian frontier. Across Cyrenaica, wrote a *Luftwaffe* General, 'mobility is restricted almost entirely to the desert road ... It is startling in the midst of this barren waste of sand and stone to fly across the tents, flocks of sheep and camels of Arabs of who no European knows ... further east you go along the desert road, the more inhospitable the landscape becomes: while about thirty miles [48km] east of Benghazi the colonizing work of the Italians is evident, around Derna and Tobruk there are no signs of human habitation ...'

BELOW: A column of vehicles from Rommel's mixed force moving along a road through Cyrenaica. One of the vehicles, a Horch Kfz 15 heavy cross-country car, can be seen towing a 3.7cm (1.45in) PaK antitank gun. Across this arid terrain, the daytime temperatures rose to over 50°C (120 °F), and at night dropped to freezing point. Apart from the terrible plagues of flies, the deadly sand vipers and scorpions, the fine sand penetrated everything the troops wore. It got into their eyes and noses, blew into tents, and choked engine filters. Sandstorms were dreaded, especially whilst moving by vehicle. In these 113km/h (70mph) storms, wheeled equipment were soon stuck up to their axles in the sand drifts. Other trucks that attempted to skirt around them also became bogged down. In some instances, tanks and other combat vehicles became stranded too, as engine oil overheated. Many men were left stranded for hours, either burning in the sun, or freezing in the dark.

ABOVE: German infantry push forward during part of the initial assault on Tobruk on 10 April 1941. The soldiers are all wearing M1935 steel helmets. Helmets issued to troops in North Africa and those countries with hot, dry climates were required to blend with the yellow sand and soil. Field-grey helmets were overpainted in a sandy-buff colour and sand was even sometimes added to the wet paint, which gave it a perfect non-reflective surface. None of the soldiers are wearing shorts as these were banned in combat areas because of injuries to legs from rocks and sand. In the foreground three soldiers can be seen with MG 34 machine guns slung over their shoulders as they move forwards, past a knocked-out vehicle.

BELOW: A group of staff officers conferring with the aid of maps the advance through the desert. The staff, headed by General Gause, was of very high quality, and very small. For instance, there were only two officers in the operations branch and three officers in the intelligence branch. The Quartermaster

Department, in charge of supplies, was commanded by one General Staff Major. Altogether with personal adjutants, the Camp Commandant, reconnaissance troops, ordnance services, and heads of engineers, repairs, and medical units, Rommel`s military staff consisted of some twenty-one officers.

ABOVE: Digging into positions near Tobruk in April 1941. A 3.7cm (1.45in) PaK 35/36 antitank gun has been set up with foliage draped over its splinter shield to afford some kind protection out in the open desert. Note one of the gunners is keeping low, protected by sandbags and the gun's shield, aware that the gun makes him a prominent target. In the

distance vehicles can be seen moving up to the front lines. The vehicle nearest the antitank gun is an SdKfz 263. Most of the vehicles deployed in the desert were camouflaged with slurry of sand and mud. For added camouflage, protection pits too were sometimes dug for the vehicles to lower their silhouettes and to give its tyres or tracks some cover.

ABOVE: Belonging to the 5th Light Division, a group of PzKpfw III medium tanks move forwards across the desert towards Tobruk. These panzers are likely to be of the Ausf G type; many were deployed in the desert, especially during the earlier part of the campaign. The PzKpfw III fought superbly and defeated all opposition in the earlier *Blitzkrieg* campaigns, despite its losses to Polish antitank guns. It was the first mass-produced version of this particular panzer type to enter service. With its 5cm (1.96in) KwK L/42 gun, it was the most potent tank in North Africa during the earlier part of 1941.

BELOW: A crew of a PzKpfw 251 south of Tobruk in May 1941. Of interest is the MG 34 mounted on top of the half-track, which has been wrapped in some canvas material in order to protect it against the desert sand. The vehicle carries a hood and, like most *Afrika Korps* vehicles, is more than likely carrying the white transverse air-recognition stripe. The vehicle has been painted with a camouflage scheme of dark sand base and carries the divisional command pennant to denote the presence of an officer. When the officer was not in the vehicle, the pennants were to removed or covered.

ABOVE: In front of three of his commanders, Rommel alters intricate details of a map in May 1941. Behind them a curious crewmember of a PzKpfw IV peers through the once-piece entry hatch on the side of the turret. In the desert, the tank was the principal weapon of war. For all tank crews that participated in Rommel's desert *Blitzkrieg* campaign, the desert was a perfect tank battlefield. Although they dreaded the thought of having their track blown off by a mine or shell, or being trapped in a blazing tank, they were an élite band of men of high spirit, built up from shared hazards and forged by comradeship. In blistering desert temperatures, the interior of a tank could become insufferably hot.

BELOW: Belonging to the 5th Panzer Regiment of the 5th Light Division – the original 'blocking force' which arrived in Tobruk in February 1941 – these vehicles have come to a halt in May 1941. On the left is a SdKfz 223. Behind it is a Volkswagen Type 82 166 Kfz 1 cross-country light personnel carrier. The third vehicle is an early production SdKfz 263 radio armoured car. Like most radio vehicles of its kind, it was equipped with a good long-range radio set with a large tubular antennae. The Signals Battalions or *Nachrichten Abteilung* were the lifeblood of any fast-moving armoured formation and in the desert the radio was widely used by the troops. These signal trucks were connected to the Divisional Headquarters.

ABOVE: British troops captured by the 8th Panzer Regiment near the Halfaya Pass being transported to the rear inside an SdKfz 251 half-track. This photograph was taken in June 1941 when the British had already launched Operation 'Brevity' under the command of Brigadier 'Strafer' Gott. British forces had successfully attacked and recaptured the Halfaya Pass. They then advanced as far as Fort Capuzzo, but were counterattacked by the *Afrika Korps* By 27 May the British had lost the Pass and were forced to withdraw. After 'Brevity' came operation 'Battleaxe' in mid-June, its sole objective to destroy Rommel's force west of Tobruk and gain a decisive victory for the British forces' commander, General Wavell. However, the *Afrika Korps* held on to the Halfaya Pass, enabling Rommel to outmanoeuvre the enemy with a brilliant, wide-sweeping counterattack.

ABOVE: Success has once more restored the situation in the desert following the failed British Operation 'Battleaxe' in mid-June 1941. Troops from the 5th Panzer Regiment have come to a halt south of Tobruk. On the right is an SdKfz 251 and on the left stands a well-laden PzKpfw III Ausf F, which is carrying a large box on the engine deck. Inside the box is the equipment needed to sustain the crew out in the harsh desert. When the *Afrika Korps* arrived in the desert, the 5th and 8th Panzer Regiments were each organized in two battalions, each of three companies. By the following year, however, they had changed their organization to three battalions, each of three companies. As it had done in Poland and France, the success of the panzer regiment in the desert depended on its deployment *en masse* and the concentration of large numbers of tanks for a deep drive into the enemy's weak areas. This *Blitzkrieg* technique was used many times to great effect against the British.

ABOVE: Tents were the most common feature of desert living in North Africa. They were very practical and easily erected. A trench was first dug, deep and wide enough to take a tent; the sides were normally strewn with sandbags to absorb sandstorms and the heavy night dew. Sand-filled tins and boxes provided the finishing touches, enabling a soldier to sleep without the prospect of his tent being blown away by the severe winds that could whip up in minutes. Living inside the tent was cramped and the worry of sand fleas, snakes and yellow scorpions was a constant fear for the men.

ABOVE: One of the best methods of erecting a tent was to construct it behind a rock face. It not only gave added protection against the harsh sandstorms, but it also offered the men some camouflage and relative safety from attack. This shows one of the ways in which the soldiers managed to quickly adapt to their unusual surroundings, for they had to fight, work, live, eat and sleep in the desert. In the heat, when not in combat, all fighting clothes were discarded, and shorts and easy lace-up shoes took their place.

RIGHT: A heavily camouflaged dug-out on the front lines in June 1941. Having chosen a piece of ground suitable either for defence or attack against tanks or assault by a mobile column, soldiers would dig in and lay sandbags, and cover their position with camouflage netting. Any foliage or rocks that could be found were also applied to the dugout for added camouflage protection. Often, especially in an advanced observation post, soldiers would wrap themselves in camouflage sheeting and bury themselves in the sand.

ABOVE: *Oberstleutnant* (Lieutenant-Colonel) Baron Irnfried von Wechmar posing for the camera inside a Horch Kfz 15 cross-country car. The picture was taken to the west of Benghazi when his 3rd Reconnaissance Battalion was given orders to advance on Benghazi along the coast. The helmet he is wearing was a conventional sun helmet that was widely issued to troops in 1941. Although not very popular among the soldiers, who almost invariably discarded it in favour of the field cap, the pith helmet continued to be worn, often behind front lines, for semi-formal occasions, including parades and ceremonies.

BELOW: Another photograph of *Oberstleutnant* von Wechmar, climbing into a vehicle with an Italian officer wearing sunglasses. This time he is wearing an army officer's tropical peaked field cap. In order to give the cap its rigid appearance, regulation woven aluminium thread piping was inserted around the entire crown seam and in the front scallop of the false flap. As with all ranks, the cap displayed the eagle and cockade badges, but with an inverted 'V' of *Waffenfarbe* soutache (braid).

ABOVE: *Oberstleutnant* von Wechmar sits among other senior officers to eat. This photograph was taken on 6 April 1941, just two days before Wechmar's reconnaissance troops, when checked north of Benghazi, had turned east by Charruba and joined in the battle at Mechili. It was at Mechili, after driving British troops out of Cyrenaica, that the troops of the 5th Light Division halted for essential maintenance. As with Rommel, Wechmar knew that success in North Africa would be solely dependent on supplies. He had made it perfectly clear to other members of his staff that the *Afrika Korps* supply line from Tripoli could be likened to a piece of elastic, liable to snap or jerk an army backwards or forwards if over-extended.

ABOVE: With the aid of a map, Rommel is directing the movements of his panzer force prior to an attack. Before an attack, the *Afrika Korps* would spend a great part of the day carrying out reconnaissance of the area, using armoured cars, small detachments of infantry and tanks. The next move was to bring up antitank guns and tanks, supported by motorized infantry, to within striking range of the enemy. By mid–afternoon, the attack would be launched with tanks moving forward – supported by fire from artillery and heavier tanks – onto the British field and antitank gun positions.

BELOW: An officer poses in front of a tent in late June 1941. He wears a typical officer's field dress, consisting of the army issue coloured mouse-grey shirt with olive-green trousers, the *Afrika Korps Feldmütze* and high, lace-up leather desert boots. The tropical shirt had two pleated breast-patch pockets, each with button-down pocket flap with two cuff buttons. The shirtsleeves were designed to be either buttoned down or rolled up, when orders stated or at an individual's choice. Behind the officer it is worth noting how deep the trench has been dug in order for a tent to be erected; most were dug only 1.2m (4ft) deep.

ABOVE: An officer and his driver from the 15th Panzer Division stop for a picnic at the side of a road. The car boot is filled with a multitude of equipment, including the officer's suitcase. The officer may have been re-posted to another unit, as it appears that most of his belongings have been stowed in the boot. The 15th Panzer Division arrived in North Africa in April 1941, just after Rommel had captured Benghazi. During 1941 soldiers of the 15th Panzer Division endured fierce and unrelenting fighting from their resilient opponents, and within months of first arriving in the desert, they had been reduced to a handful of operational tanks that were eventually compelled to be withdrawn for re-fitting. It was not until January of the following year that further reinforcements allowed the division to go onto the offensive again.

RIGHT: Abandoned British positions in mid-June 1941 near Sollum. It was at Sollum in the scorching heat and through choking dust clouds that a bloody and violent tank and infantry battle raged. Despite fighting against an uneven weight of armour, Rommel's superior tactics, coupled with the stubborn resistance of German and Italian troops, brought a much-needed victory. For miles, the wreckage of battle was strewn across the desert, including the dead from both sides. In this photograph intact ammunition boxes have been left behind, including an assortment of rifles and other battle souvenirs.

ABOVE: A flak unit observation team as part of the support and subsidiary units of the 15th Panzer Division survey the sky. They have spotted an aircraft, but their calm nature tells us that it is German. An antiaircraft battalion usually comprised two heavy batteries, each of four 8.8cm (3.45in) towed guns, and one light battery of 2cm (0.78in) and 3.7cm (1.45in) guns.

BELOW: Members of an *Afrika Korps* regiment take time out to relax beneath a canopy. This photograph was taken in late June 1941, when many of the soldiers were in the 'Cairo spirit', confident of their ultimate success. It is clear from this picture that the men are now more acclimatized to the desert conditions. Late that summer, the *Afrika Korps* was further strengthened and renamed *Panzergruppe Afrika*. It now boasted six Italian divisions, 15th and 21st Panzer Divisions, and the 90th Light Division, which included units of the 5th Light Division. Total strength numbered some 55,000 men.

RIGHT: A well-tended German war grave south of Tobruk in June 1941. Tobruk was the most important port in North Africa and with the town occupied by the British, Rommel was determined to capture it at all costs. But Tobruk was defended by some of the British Empire's toughest troops and they were ready to fight, alnmost to the death. The first battle for Tobruk was a complete disaster for Rommel, with the loss of hundreds of his finest troops. He grudgingly accepted that the defenders needed to be worn down with relentless bombardments, so he bypassed Tobruk and pushed most of his men on to Sollum.

LEFT: Under a baking-hot midday sun, two officers, one wearing a pair of field binoculars, survey a map and the landscape around them. Both men are wearing the same type of tropical field service tunic and *Feldmütze* headgear, except it would seem that the officer on the right is in fact wearing a white tunic. This white appearance is obviously caused by the bleaching effects of the sun. The same officer appears to have added the hand-embroidered silver breast eagle from the continental uniform to his tunic, but retained the tropical collar patches. Both these uniforms are of early manufacture, with pleated pockets under scalloped flaps.

ABOVE: Two faces of the Axis – an Italian and a German officer relax together in the shade of a truck, escaping from the sun's heat. Relations between the Germans and their allies varied. Some Italian formations were recognized as being the equal of German units, particularly formations like the *Ariete* Division. Unfortunately even the most motivated of Italian units tended to use inferior equipment to both their German allies and their Allied enemies. One example of this was the M13/40 tank, which was poorly-armoured, undergunned, and slow and unreliable. Large numbers were destroyed or captured by the Allies during their advance in 1940, and no suitable replacement was available. Other Italian formations were less reliable, and tended to be used as support formations for better-equipped and more motivated German units.

ABOVE: From an open field store a motorcyclist is about to load an army-issue sack, containing a tent, onto his motorcycle combination. Such combinations were adapted to carry an MG 34 as well as the motorcycle battalion's smaller guns. Although strictly not allowed to carry oversized and heavy objects, riders did at their own peril. Out in the desert, the motorcycle was particularly flexible and fast-moving, suitable for racing across the arid terrain to occupy important features and engaging weak enemy forces. They were very well suited, especially during the night, to supporting an armoured attack. In North Africa a motorcycle battalion contained an HQ, three rifle companies, an MG company, and a heavy company. All were equipped with same type of weapons as the Panzergrenadier battalions, but with a total of some 271 motorcycles.

RIGHT: On 18 November 1941 Rommel returned from a holiday with his wife in Rome to Africa. This rare photograph was taken at Gambut, where his new *Panzergruppe Afrika* (Panzer Group Africa) was headquartered. The sky that day was grey, it was cold, and it had been raining. In fact, torrential rivers had appeared, carrying away tents, equipment, and even troops. To make matters worse, shifting sands were disrupted by the moving water, causing mines to explode, which consequently overturned passing vehicles and caused a number of fatal casualties. In this bad weather, Rommel was handed reports that the British had begun wide, sweeping movements north-west of Fort Maddalena on the Egyptian border. Unknown to Rommel, these movements were the beginning of the British offensive, Operation 'Crusader'. But for some reason, for the first time, Rommel's fabled 'sixth sense' at detecting the advance of the enemy had failed him. In fact, initially he did not even believe the British had unleashed a full-scale offensive. While he debated the enemy's movements, the enemy was using the same methods of attack that Rommel had used so often and repeatedly in the desert. A quick, decisive lightning attack, a rapid flank movement with unabated ferocity, and a deep, penetrating strike into the enemy's main arteries: all were now being brought to bear against the 'Desert Fox'.

ABOVE: A knocked-out British Matilda tank during Operation 'Crusader' in November 1941. Across an area of desert of about 129km² (50 square miles) from the Egyptian frontier in the east, to the road south out of Tobruk in the west, tanks fought tanks. Soon the battlefield was littered with the dead and burnt-out hulks of armoured vehicles. With staggering losses, Rommel managed to blunt the British offensive. Although his men were outnumbered against excellently armed and equipped soldiers, he was determined to prevent the British hammering a corridor through to Tobruk, and willing to commit more men to battle.

BELOW: A Horch Kfz 15 light cross-country vehicle has halted in the desert. The licence plate on the car's right mudguard is WH702460. Except for tanks, full-tracked vehicles and self-propelled weapons, all German vehicles carried these licence plates. They were the military identification number for the majority of vehicles in service, and carried letter prefix groups to indicate the organization to which the vehicle was assigned. The military letter groupings denoted the major components of the *Wehrmacht*. The first two letters 'WH', denoted it as belonging to the *Wehrmacht Heere* or Army.

LEFT: Another view of the British Matilda tank, knocked out by a direct hit from an antitank gun. Out in the desert the Antitank Battalion, or *Panzerjäger Abteilung* (motorized), was very effective against British tanks and scored sizeable successes during a battle. An antitank battalion consisted of 3 companies, a light ammunition column of 10 lorries, and a light supply column of some 20 lorries. Each company contained a light platoon of at least four 3.7cm (1.45in) antitank guns, and two medium platoons, each with three 5cm (1.96in) antitank guns. Each battalion had 12 3.7cm and 18 5cm antitank guns.

ABOVE: A well dug-in tent south of Tobruk in January 1942. Earth and sandbags have been used to protect the sides of the tent, and rocks have been placed on the roof to prevent it from being damaged or even blown away by a sandstorm. A *Zeltbahn* has been put to good use in order to protect the entrance and to keep it dry. When soldiers were short of tents, they would use the well-tested method of combining a number of *Zeltbahnen* to form two- or four-man 'pup' tents.

CHAPTER SEVEN

Last Throw

The End of the Desert *Blitzkrieg*

Despite Rommel's retreat across nearly 482km (300 miles) of desert, his forces had withdrawn without serious loss, and were still able to inflict considerable damage on the enemy. As ever undeterred, Rommel was determined to launch a new offensive. First he was going to re-supply, rehabilitate and reorganize his forces, then he planned to lay 100,000 mines in a new line.

LEFT: A water-point near Mersa El Brega in January 1942. Empty jerry cans are being filled with water for passing vehicles. No amount was enough for the troops on marches of hundreds of miles.

FAR LEFT: An Arab volunteer in Tunisia in January 1943. The Vichy Government organized Arabs, North Africans and even French citizens into the Africa Phalanx, a force of 400 men, to support the *Afrika Korps*.

During the first weeks of January 1942, Rommel tirelessly inspected his units which were digging in along the lines at Mersa El Brega. For days he brooded over maps, photographs and intelligence reports, preparing his panzer group, not for defence, but a surprise attack on the enemy. Back home the Reich held its breath as Rommel began preparing for another offensive that would lead him to victory. His reputation in Germany had grown to new heights, with the radios blaring out waves of exaltation for their 'Desert Fox'. He now needed to deliver to the German people another spectacular victory that would raise both public morale and military confidence. Finally, after weeks of preparation, on 21 January 1942, Rommel's surprise attack began in earnest.

ROMMEL ADVANCES

Almost immediately the *Afrika Korps* outwitted, outmanoeuvred and outgunned their bewildered enemy. Wilfred Armbruster, Rommel's new interpreter, wrote: 'The Tommies don't stand and fight. They have just turned and fled.' Within five days, the Germans had knocked out and captured 299 enemy tanks and armoured fighting vehicles and 147 guns, and they had taken 935 prisoners. The British were now in full retreat, and the smouldering port of Benghazi once again changed hands. In just two weeks, Rommel had bulldozed halfway back across Cyrenaica,

and for this success Hitler promoted him to Colonel-General. With Hitler's faith in him now restored, Rommel was eager to reconquer all Cyrenaica, capture Tobruk, and advance on Egypt and the Nile.

In April, after a lull in the fighting, Rommel secretly re-shuffled his panzer army to prepare them for an attack on the British Gazala line, which ran down from the coast into the desert, 64km (40 miles) west of Tobruk. He knew that this well-fortified defence line, already boasting half a million mines, was not going to be easy to crack. But he knew that the British field army must be destroyed, and Tobruk captured first. For this reason he chose the exceptionally daring plan of sending his army's entire tank strength on an outflanking move round the southern end of the Gazala line to dupe the enemy. Then he was going to drive north and capture Tobruk. The plan was so bold, he knew that if it failed, he stood to lose all Africa. But such a daring plan was too irresistible for the 'Desert Fox' to ignore. Tobruk would be captured at any cost.

On 26 May 1942, X-Day for the attack began. Rommel's entire striking force of 10,000 vehicles moved south against the setting sun. What followed was complete chaos: the British suddenly attacked. By the following day one-third of Rommel's armour had been lost. A few days later, wild rumours were spreading that the British had encircled the *Afrika Korps* and that Rommel was dead.

RIGHT: Late December 1941, a motorcycle combination and Opel-Blitz trucks wind down a hillside near Mersa El Brega during the *Afrika Korps'* withdrawal from Cyrenaica. At the end of November, the British lines once again stiffened and, with further reinforcements, began streaming towards Rommel's exhausted and overstretched lines. With no fuel or ammunition left, Rommel ordered a general retreat from Cyrenaica. On Christmas Day, Benghazi was recaptured by the British, and by early 1942 the *Afrika Korps* was back to where it had begun the previous spring.

But soon the 'Desert Fox' established radio contact with his headquarters, and there now seemed a glimmer of hope. Still undaunted by the British, he pushed his forces forwards through the minefield and closed in around the heavily defended town of Bir Hakeim. For eight days, completely surrounded, the 1st Free French Brigade held out valiantly until they finally capitulated. The British Eighth Army, now in danger of being encircled, attempted to fall back to Tobruk. Rommel was free to wheel northwards through the disintegrating Gazala Line, infusing his masterly tactics with one crushing blow after another. He advanced with twice the number of tanks as the British, his path leading inevitably to Tobruk

On 18 June, Rommel moved in to take his prize. While his forces massed outside the perimeter and surrounded the port, Stukas pounded it mercilessly. Then, as the massive aerial bombardment subsided, the *Afrika Korps* and the 20th Italian Corps saturated the town with hundreds of artillery pieces. By 21 June Tobruk finally surrendered. Back at home the Reich was intoxicated with the news of Tobruk's surrender. On 22 June, from Hitler's East Prussian headquarters, the Führer promoted Rommel to the rank of Field Marshal. With the fall of Tobruk, and the British fleeing across the desert, victory for Rommel seemed only a matter of time.

EL ALAMEIN

By July 1942, Rommel was only 62km (100 miles) from the great British naval base at Alexandria. In Cairo, a state of emergency had been declared. With the air of a victorious warlord, Rommel now ventured into unknown terrain, leading his troops in broad formation against the well-fortified town of El Alamein. Throughout July and the first half of August, the 'Desert Fox' pounded away at the El Alamein position. But the Eighth Army repeatedly thwarted Rommel's attempts to crush their strong defences. After 17 months of battling across the desert, Rommel's army was wearying under the strain, and his health was faltering. He was 16,000 men below strength, and sickness amongst the troops was reaching epidemic proportions. For the attack against El Alamein, he could only field 203 panzers against 767 of Montgomery's tanks. Despite the depletion of supplies and the overwhelming numbers of British troops, on 30 August he prepared his men for one last attempt to bulldoze through enemy positions and into the very heart of Egypt.

All along the German front, under the pale moonlight, Rommel's armour began its attack, moving eastward through minefields which were stubbornly defended by infantry equipped with artillery, guns and mortars. It was evident to Rommel, judging by the stiff resistance, that Montgomery, the new Allied commander, had been expecting the attack and was prepared for it. In the mayhem and confusion that engulfed everyone, both panzer divisions lost their commanders, and were brought to a flaming halt. Lieutenant General Nehring of the 15th had been severely injured by air attack, and Major General von Bismarck of the 21st had been killed by a mine.

It seemed that enemy air power and the brilliant defensive use of artillery were the deciding factor in Rommel's loss of control on the battlefield. On 23 October, Montgomery finally brought the climatic showdown at El Alamein to a head. With a devastating artillery barrage, the British surged forward in a ferocious attack. The Germans who took the brunt of its fury called it 'Desert Armageddon'. Within one week, after throwing in his last reserves, Rommel was fighting for survival. He had lost the battle at El Alamein.

By 3 November, Rommel had only 35 panzers left at his disposal. Not even waiting for word from Hitler, he now took his fate into his own hands and ordered the retreat of his beloved *Afrika Korps*. For Rommel, there would be no more *Blitzkrieg* tactics. Instead, he now faced a harrowing retreat back across the vast desert, carrying a remarkable amount of more than 70,000 German and Italian troops with him. Field Marshal Erwin Rommel, who had dominated the battlefield, who had been bold in attack, ferocious in pursuit of the enemy, and obsessed with obtaining his objective, had finally met his match. The threat of the 'Desert Fox' in Africa had once and for all finally been vanquished.

RIGHT: The withdrawal of Rommel's forces continues. A motorcycle combination and an Opel-Blitz truck pass under a triumphal arch built by the Italians on the Via Balba. The Germans withdrew across nearly 482 km (300 miles) of desert without great losses and were still able to inflict serious injury on its enemy. But despite the *Afrika Korps'* retreat, Rommel remained as determined as ever, and eagerly set about planning a new offensive. First he was going to re-supply, rehabilitate and reorganize his forces, and then he would lay 100,000 mines in a new defence line in Tripolitania. Follwong this, he would strike east once again and move towards the Egyptian frontier.

ABOVE: Two commanders discuss the next strategic move while an Italian officer looks on. The vehicle passing behind the group of officers is a Kfz 15 Horch light cross-country car. While preparations were made for the new defence line at Mersa el Brega, the Italian command took advantage of the rest period to reorganize its two infantry corps. The *Afrika Korps* intended to have these two Italian infantry corps in position, and to leave the mobile formations in the rear. The bulk of the Italian infantry were ordered to stand in the northern sector of the new defence line to act purely in a counterattacking role.

ABOVE: Along the coast near Benghazi captured British troops sit on a beach waiting to be transported to the rear as PoWs. They will be shipped back to mainland Europe as soon as possible, to reduce the drain on the *Afrika Korps'* resources. The desert war was a 'gentlemanly' war, with both sides treating prisoners well. Undoubtedly the common enemy, the climate of the North African desert, provided a strong bond between the two sides. Both the Allies and the Axis troops preferred fighting by the sea, where the opportunity of cooling down in the Mediterranean existed. Further inland, towards the heart of the Sahara, temperatures soared.

BELOW: On an airstrip Junkers Ju52s are transporting injured soldiers back to Italy following a number of heavy casualties during the successful attack by Rommel in late January 1942. Around Benghazi, Derna and Martuba, German air formations quickly occupied all the landing strips, undoubtedly bringing an improvement in the supply situation. German air power increased, and more supplies reached North Africa throughout February 1942, allowing a smoother replenishment of men and materiel, and encouraging the Panzer Army to launch a new offensive. However, there was a grave shortage in equipment, and supply was still unsatisfactory.

LEFT: Accompanied by his staff, in tropical uniform, Rommel salutes as he carries on his way to prepare plans for further attacks against the British. This photograph was taken in July 1942, a few weeks after Rommel had been promoted to *Generalfeldmarschall* (Field Marshal) by Hitler at the Wolf's Lair. By July 1942 Rommel was only 62km (100 miles) from the great British naval base at Alexandria. In Cairo a state of emergency had been declared. With the air of a victorious warlord, the 'Desert Fox' now planned to venture into unknown territory and capture the well-fortified town of El Alamein.

ABOVE: A small formal parade of *Afrika Korps* soldiers stand to attention and raise their Mauser rifles to the salute of their commanding officer. The troops are wearing the peaked *Feldmütze* cap and are dressed in typical clothing worn by soldiers during a formal ceremony in 1942: tropical tunic with shirt and tie, tropical breeches and boots. These men are about to receive some kind of decoration for their bravery or marksmanship on the battlefield.

LEFT: Rommel confers with one of his staff. He was often seen standing in his command car; his constant presence on the front lines was an inspiration to his men and the key to his leadership. Rommel always wanted to see action and he directed it personally from the front, changing tactics as the battle flowed and ebbed. By June 1942 Rommel's force had surged some 965km (600 miles) east and was no more than 97km (60 miles) from Alexandria. With victory in sight, he now ordered his troops onwards to attack the El Alamein position.

LEFT: Rommel, with his personal *Afrika Korps* staff, surveys the endless terrain ahead. Note the commander to Rommel's right wearing the famous *Afrika Korps* cuff band sewn onto his greatcoat. Behind Rommel is a group of Italian officers. The 'Desert Fox' had little time for Italian senior officers, but had a paternal way with their soldiers. Although the language barrier made for obvious communication problems, Rommel's drive, energy, and sheer presence helped turn around the Italian Army's low morale. Out in the desert, Rommel was able to see far beyond his front-line positions and track Allied movements.

ABOVE: Rommel confers with his staff inside his command car, briefing them about the tactics he has chosen for the ensuing battle. This was a frequent sight, for Rommel preferred to sit in the front of his car with his driver, rather than at the back; from this vantage point, he could scrutinize the landscape as he passed through. With the aid of a map, at every outpost the *Feldmarschall* would get out of his car to make endless surveys of the area. He would then clamber back into the vehicle and would proceed to pore over the map, trying to formulate a masterstroke against his Allied foes.

BELOW: Rommel stands in his command car while a member of his staff briefs his officers. Rommel was, without doubt, a master tactician. His officers and personal staff soon recognized a commanding intelligence of rare capacity. Although Rommel's tactical plans were sometimes over-ambitious, his *Blitzkrieg* advance through the desert was supported by the authorities in both Rome and Berlin. With Rommel's strength boosted by the rich pickings of Tobruk, he eagerly exploited his victory. He believed in denying the enemy any respite; that adopting the offensive rather that continuing to strengthen his positions at Mersa El Brega was the only way of securing a rapid victory. El Alamein was one of those few positions in the desert where the front, due to the terrain, prevented outflanking manoeuvres. Cliffs and escarpments offered the British the chance to fight.

RIGHT: The attack on El Alamein is finally unleashed. Rommel and his staff train their eyes as vehicles push forwards to the front lines. On 13 July 1942 the 21st Panzer Division carried out a coordinated attack with tanks and infantry, which, due to heavy enemy artillery fire, was soon blunted. Three days later the 21st Panzer Division experienced the problem again. The first battle of Alamein did not begin until 21 July, when coordinated armour counterattacked, with severe losses of Allied troops. For Rommel, who watched the battle slowly unfold from his command car, it was a critical moment in the campaign in North Africa.

LEFT: Rommel inside his Kfz 15 mE medium standard passenger car during the battle of El Alamein. Out in the desert the sun's rays were scorching, especially at midday. The vehicle's canopy can clearly be seen raised to reduce the temperature and prevent dust from penetrating the vehicle. These were trying times for the 'Desert Fox', and he knew that British strength was increasing all the time. His staff estimated that by 20 August 1942, the enemy would have over 900 tanks, 850 antitank guns and 550 guns. Rommel only had just over 500 tanks. The threat of defeat was now staring him right in the face.

ABOVE: The most essential asset of an army for the effective continuation of war is an adequate stock of weapons, ammunition and fuel. In this photograph *Afrika Korps* troops are unloading large drums of fuel from a captured British fuel supply train. Some of the railway carriages appear to have been subjected to an aerial attack which has derailed the trains' engine. Supplying troops in the desert was the most vital element of the war in Africa for both sides. The line of supply for either force stretched some 644km (400 miles) from its main base. For the Axis, it was Tripoli, and for the Allies, Alexandria. However both sides when they were advancing stretched their supply lines to the limit, before sufficient intermediate supply bases could be established. Consequently, they found themselves overstretched and undersupplied. Unable to hold their positions in the face of an enemy with shortened supply lines, they were forced to withdraw.

RIGHT: A German soldier takes a photograph of a sign erected by the British in Egypt, naming the route after Wavell, the former Allied commander in the region. After the area's capture by the *Afrika Korps*, the sign has been altered to 'Rommel Way' in honour of its new owners. Wavell had had mixed success against Rommel, as had his successor, Auchinleck, but soon the Allies were to have a new commander in the desert, General Bernard Law Montgomery. Like Rommel, an inspiring commander, Montgomery was to meet the famed 'Desert Fox' in battle for the first time at El Alamein.

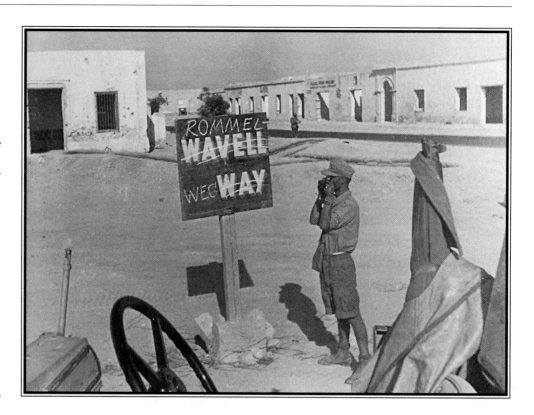

ABOVE: An intermediate supply base stationed in the middle of the desert. These supply lines were the main artery to any army wishing to sustain itself in North Africa. However, due to RAF activity during August 1942, German supplies were reduced by some 20 per cent. Rommel's supply problems were even further multiplied by the lack of spare parts for the *Afrika Korps'* numerous trucks. As many as 80 per cent of them were captured British vehicles; only a small amount of German and Italian trucks were slowly arriving. In fact, the logistical problems that August had become dire. Troops were short of food, and bread rations were halved as a consequence. By mid–August, the *Afrika Korps'* held between 8 and 10 days of ammunition, and only enough fuel to take a panzer division some 97km (60 miles) over three days.

ABOVE: *Afrika Korps* officers survey the terrain ahead. In the distance, armoured vehicles protected by high ground wait before resuming their advance. The vehicle on the right appears to be an antiaircraft flak gun mounted on the back of a half-track artillery tractor. This is probably the very effective 2cm (0.78in) Flak 38, mounted on a 3.08 tonne (3 ton) Demag D7. This weapon was primarily used in the desert to pin down the infantry following up behind a tank attack. It weighed 1509kg (3327lb) and its muzzle velocity was 900m/s (2951ft/s), with a maximum ceiling of 2200m (2407yd).

ABOVE: Captured British, French and colonial troops pass by in a dishevelled state, marching to the rear to begin a new and arduous existence as PoWs. It is of interest to note the variety of clothing being worn by the soldiers, especially those from the colonial forces. A number of the men are wearing pre-1940 French greatcoats and French steel helmets. But it is particularly worth noting the soldier in the centre, who is wearing the full French Foreign Legion campaign dress.

ABOVE: On the coast, aircraft are bringing more supplies into North Africa. Parked at the side of the airstrip is an SdKfz 7 half-track. Throughout the African campaign, air-freighting was used to cut down on the transportation of supplies by sea. This was arguably the greatest and most effective way in logistical support. Not only did it save thousands of tonnes of supplies from being sent to the bottom of the sea by enemy shipping, but it also reduced the demand for road transport from ports like Tripoli, Benghazi and Tobruk. Road transport over huge distances on indifferent surfaces consumed lots of fuel, therefore every mile travelled increased the demand on Rommel's fast-diminishing fuel supplies.

ABOVE: Off-duty soldiers gather round a tent south of El Alamein in the summer of 1942, listening to a radio. Like so many soldiers fighting far away from home, the men of the *Afrika Korps* sought bonds of comradeship and were determined to make the most of what little leisure was available to them. By this time the *Afrika Korps* was lacking in entertainment and food rations had been halved. While spending short periods out of action, the men generated their own forms of amusement. Some played chess, using various bullets as pieces, while others read old newspapers and magazines.

BELOW: A group of decorated officers share a private joke as one of the men, wearing field binoculars and holding the rank of major, handles a turtle in the desert. Various styles of German Army tropical clothing can be seen in this picture. The major is wearing the tropical version of what was very similar to the motorcyclist's rubberized coat. Not to be confused with the standard tropical greatcoat made from dark-brown woollen cloth, this particular coat was manufactured in an olive colour similar to that of the tropical field blouse. Double-breasted, this coat featured two large side pockets.

ABOVE: A captured British armoured car belonging to an *Afrika Korps* signals battalion has come to a halt inside an encampment. Armoured signals vehicles accompanied the advancing tanks wherever they went, and supplied the communications necessary for the commanders to control their forces effectively. Radio was used extensively in the desert, since landlines were time-consuming to lay. Every command vehicle had a receiving set, and every artillery troop had sets with one principal frequency for emergency use. Radio vehicles were equipped with long-range sets, a vital asset in the desert.

RIGHT: North Africans pose for the camera as an officer on top of his Volkswagen type 82 Kfz 1 peers across the arid desert through his binoculars. Depending on the terrain factor, soldiers were able to see on a very clear day 40km (25 miles) across the desert. The *Afrika Korps* made full use of the freedom of manoeuvre which desert terrain allowed. The lack of terrain obstacles and the use of armoured units compared to those of the *Blitzkrieg* campaign in Poland and in Western Europe gave the spearheads the chance to advance in several columns, using wide, sweeping manoeuvres to defeat the enemy whenever possible.

RIGHT: An engineer battalion post in the Western Desert in the summer of 1942. The engineer can be seen wearing a pith helmet and the basic uniform worn by the *Afrika Korps*. The primary task of this engineer was to keep the division mobile, which included locating and clearing obstacles, marking minefields and clearing lanes through them to enable the armour to pour through. Where a minefield was to be forced open, the engineers would locate mines by prodding the ground with bayonets or with mine detectors. The mines were then carefully removed and a gap forced and marked. This was the method by which the Allied defences at Tobruk were broken down.

ABOVE: Soldiers from a signals battalion with their lightweight radio set (Torn.Fu.bl) and large 'T' aerial out in the desert. This was probably a forward observation post, from where they were probably sending the Divisional Headquarters various messages, including grid references on which they had to fire or send their armoured units into attack. These radio sets were vital and enabled the user to signal traffic and pass vital intelligence to the operational staff.

ABOVE: Two crewmembers are standing next to their PzKpfw III out in the open desert. This particular panzer type was used as the main striking force in the campaign in North Africa. It had a dominant role in tank-against-tank combat. With its powerful 5cm (1.96in) gun, it had the advantage over all types of tanks it had encountered in the desert. As with previous *Blitzkrieg* campaigns, the PzKpfw III demonstrated its effectiveness at overrunning enemy positions with speed and manouevrability, and used its gun as artillery against forward enemy columns with devastating effect.

BELOW: Preparing for the battle of El Alamein, the soldiers of the *Afrika Korps* anxiously wait to move forwards. An SdKfz 251 and PzKpfw III Ausf G are poised to begin action in one of the boldest attempts made by Rommel to crush his British opponents. The half-track has a wheel attached to its front, probably for added armoured protection. The panzer has also been given armoured protection by the track links attached to its front and side. The Ausf G is identifiable by the bolt flange around the mantlet and machinegun ball mount to which the waterproof fabric cover is attached.

ABOVE: On the move is a Pz.Kpfw III Ausf G belonging to the 21st Panzer Division. The basic tank regiment had altered three times between the start of the campaign in February 1941 and mid–1942. Each tank regiment contained a total of 204 panzers, of which 136 were light armoured combat vehicles or *Panzer Kampfwagens* (tanks), consisting of PzKpfw Is and IIs, and only 68 medium and heavy PzKpfw III and IVs. By 1942 most PzKpw Is had been phased out and the tank regiment organized into three battalions, each of three companies comprised of 201 tanks. There were 68 PzKpfw IIs, 102 PzKpfw IIIs and 30 PzKpfw IVs. The battalions were divided into two light tank companies and one medium tank company.

LEFT A PzKpfw III Ausf G racing across the desert. The sand is being churned up by the tank's tracks, creating large amounts of billowing dust clouds that could be seen for miles. Out in the desert, frontal tank assaults were not often deployed in offensive tactics: main attacks were directed against one or both flanks. Panzer tactics, particularly those employed by PzKpw IIIs, usually began with opening fire at about 1600m (1750yd), which was normally beyond the effective range of hostile weapons. Once contact had been made, the speed of advance was immediately reduced, but its 5cm (1.96in) guns were still used in order to keep enemy tanks out of range. Its main objective was to knock out the antitank guns and all visible field guns.

RIGHT: Climbing a sand dune this PzKpfw III Ausf G uses its powerful engine to overcome the high gradient. Several stick-grenades can be seen mounted on the side of the turret. Water bottles are attached to the rear turret. The crew have stowed a number of items over the engine deck, including a box full of supplies and rolled-up canvas sheeting which, when pulled over the top of the tank and tied down, formed a kind of canopy and broke up the outlines of the tank. The canopy was primarily used to protect the crew from enemy attack by disguising it as a truck. The bleached canvas covered with a threaded screen was stretched taut from a central position on the tank's turret at an angle of not more than 45 degrees, before being attached to the ground with pegs.

ABOVE: Destroyed fishing boats lie on the shore of the Mediterranean after being attacked by Royal Air Force bombers. The majority of attacks unleashed by the might of the RAF in late 1942 were carried out from airstrips in Egypt and Malta.

Thousands of tonnes of German supply ships continued to be sunk by the RAF. These aerial attacks caused considerable damage to large parts of the North African coastline, including Tripoli, Benghazi and Tobruk.

ABOVE: An MG 34 machine gun crew overlooking positions near El Alamein in September 1942. Next to the gunner, or *Schütze* 1, is his team-mate, *Schütze* 2. It was his duty to feed the ammunition belts and ensure that the gun remained clean and operational. The MG 34 was a formidable weapon of war. It weighed 12.1kg (26.67lb) and had a maximum muzzle velocity of 762m/s (2500ft/s). Its magazine capacity was a 75-round drum or 250-round belts. Note the gunners' optical sight on the sustained fire mount; there is a mechanical linkage to the trigger on the gun, so as he fires the gun using the grip trigger. A well-sighted, well-hidden and well-supplied MG 34 could hold up an entire attacking regiment. The machine-gun nest is perfectly sited on top of a rock face, and could inflict heavy losses on any enemy advance.

RIGHT: A well-camouflaged 3.7cm (1.45in) PaK antitank gun is sited on a position south of El Alamein. The gunner peers through his binoculars, trying to deduce the firing range of his target. In the desert, almost every gun was dug into a pit and covered with a net. A gun pit that had no parapet and was flush with the surface of the ground was better concealed than one that had a parapet. Like the vehicles, artillery pieces would also receive a liberal application of dull, yellow sand-coloured paint. Covered with a camouflage net and using pieces of foliage and sandmats, the artillery would blend well into the sandy terrain.

ABOVE: Sited among some rocks, a soldier has dug a small foxhole to conceal himself from the enemy. Quick concealment from both ground and air was obtained by digging a foxhole where a soldier could live for a number of days. This soldier's entrenching tool can be seen next to his foxhole. The main concern in selecting a position was the suitability of the soil for digging, and the possibility of keeping in contact with other soldiers in his unit for mutual support. In this case a rocky outcrop has given the *Afrika Korps* soldier concealment but a difficult surface to dig.

ABOVE: A variety of armoured vehicles and tanks plough through the open desert using the famous *Afrika Korps* 'V' formation. A battalion of about 75 tanks usually used this formation, with two companies leading and one in reserve. These companies in line, with tanks in column, were normally found at about 55m (60yd) intervals and advanced in waves, with four or six tanks in depth. The panzer battalion moved in short rushes, taking advantage of the wide-open terrain. The relatively close formation was more readily controlled than a wide, sweeping one. Despite the rapid advance, field artillery and antitank weapons were kept as close as possible. From the air, it was a truly impressive sight to see dozens of vehicles tearing across the desert with sand dust billowing out behind them. In fact, these vehicles were easy targets, and yet some RAF pilots seemed to hesitate from attacking German tank formations in the forward areas.

ABOVE: An antitank gun being used in action at the end of August 1942. An antitank battalion consisted of three companies, with each company containing a light platoon of four 3.7cm (1.45in) antitank guns, and two medium platoons, each with three 5cm (1.96in) antitank guns. Because of its speed and mobility across country, the antitank battalion was a very formidable unit. In defence the average frontage it covered ranged about 400m x 400m (437yd x 437yd). On the offensive it usually defended the flanks, but it could also attack enemy armour with deadly effect.

ABOVE: Across the vast, sprawling, treeless landscape, waiting for the enemy, is an MG 34 machine gun crew using the optical sight on the MG-Lafatte 34 sustained-fire mount. The photograph illustrates well the fact that not all the fighting was conducted on flat, featureless terrain. The MG 34 was the main infantry-support weapon that first saw action in Poland in 1939. The mount gave the machine gun sufficient stability to reach a maximum range of 2000m (2187yd).

RIGHT: A 15cm (5.9in) sFH18 in its firing position near El Alamein in September 1942. In command of the battery is a Technical Sergeant, who can be seen on the left. Dust is still evident from the last shot at enemy positions. Another projectile has been pushed forcefully into the barrel with the long rammer, followed by the cartridge case with the specified number of charges. In a panzer division there were usually three fully mechanized batteries in an artillery regiment: two field batteries of 12 10.5cm (4.1in) gun howitzers, and one medium battery with one troop of four 10.5cm (4.1in) guns and two of four 15cm (5.9in) gun howitzers.

ABOVE: By raising his arm, the artillery commander signals for the gun crew to fire. Many types of guns were used by the *Afrika Korps*, including large numbers of captured British guns, and Russian field artillery pieces which had been brought to North Africa from the Eastern Front. Since speed was essential out in the desert, the artillery commander needed to make sure that his planning was careful and timely. In this way, he could ensure that his guns would give the most rapid direct support to the panzers, and that they would be able to follow their advance as quickly as possible.

LEFT: British tanks have been hit and destroyed by strong German defensive positions. German defensive tactics were unique. Barrages were laid in front of the most advanced defensive positions and a screen of fire was used to protect them from attacking infantry and tanks. During these heavy sustained bombardments, lanes were purposely left open to allow German patrols to operate during the attack. The most effective German defensive weapon during the North African campaign was the 8.8cm (3.45in) Flak 18 heavy gun. Specifically designed for a dual role, it possessed an antitank capability. At 2000m (2189yd) the gun was capable of penetrating 132mm (5.2in), which proved very successful.

BELOW: A captured British Morris C8 4 x 4 'Quad' field artillery tractor used for towing field guns and ammunition limbers. This particular Morris is towing a British 25-pounder (87.6mm (3.45in)), which was more than capable of knocking out light and medium tanks. A number of these guns and armoured vehicles were used by the *Afrika Korps* against their former owners.

ABOVE: Signals engineers are setting up overhead telephone lines. Almost all the lines used by the *Afrika Korps* when they first arrived in Africa were laid on the ground. However, the amount of traffic passing over them caused them to become damaged and sometimes severed. It was therefore agreed that the most desirable way of avoiding this damage was for the lines to be erected overhead. Such a system permitted the various commands to pass orders effectively out in the field and at the same time eliminate any risk of their communications being overheard by the enemy.

ABOVE: An MG 34 machine-gun crew perched on the side of a mountain with a wide-open view of the terrain below. The MG 34 was the world's first general-purpose machine gun and could be used in both a heavy- and a light role. It had an effective range of 2000m (2188yd). A well-sighted, well-supplied MG 34 on a frontage of several miles was more than capable of mowing down dozens of attacking enemy soldiers, and holding the rest up for hours. Although it had one major drawback – rapid overheating with sustained fire – it remained an impressive weapon, and was manufactured until 1945.

RIGHT: Soldiers are seen readily bartering for eggs and other delicacies from the local people of a small town. On the whole, the Germans treated the locals in North Africa with a degree of respect. Enticed by the cheap prices offered to them, the soldiers often purchased all forms of goods, including gifts for home – all readily supplied by the local traders. Being offered the chance to eat eggs and other foods in scarce supply, due to rationing, was always alluring for them, especially after provisions in the later part of the campaign had become so mundane and monotonous.

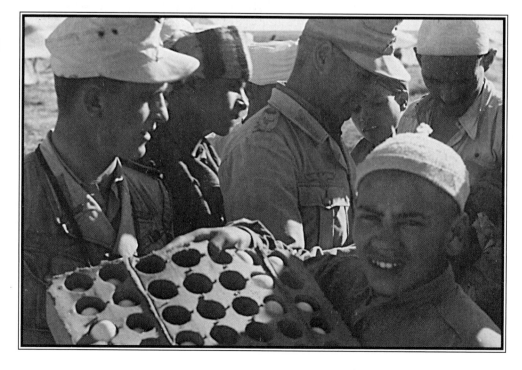

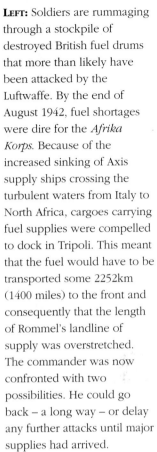

LEFT: Soldiers are rummaging through a stockpile of destroyed British fuel drums that more than likely have been attacked by the Luftwaffe. By the end of August 1942, fuel shortages were dire for the *Afrika Korps*. Because of the increased sinking of Axis supply ships crossing the turbulent waters from Italy to North Africa, cargoes carrying fuel supplies were compelled to dock in Tripoli. This meant that the fuel would have to be transported some 2252km (1400 miles) to the front and consequently that the length of Rommel's landline of supply was overstretched. The commander was now confronted with two possibilities. He could go back – a long way – or delay any further attacks until major supplies had arrived.

LEFT: This photograph, taken in early October 1942, shows soldiers looking out across the Mediterranean. They are probably privately wondering when they will return home and see their families and loved ones. But already the beginning of the end had materialized for the *Afrika Korps*. Not only were they seriously curtailed by the lack of supplies reaching the front, but the balance of numbers was also strongly in favour of the Allies. Although the Germans had succeeded in constructing formidable defensive positions 16km (10 miles) in depth, and were protected by over five million mines planted in what was known as 'Rommel's Devil's Gardens', they were some 2252km (1400 miles) distant from Tripoli, with their supply lines overstretched to the point of snapping.

LEFT: High up on the minaret of a mosque is an *Afrika Korps* observation post. The men have also erected a wire to get a good reception from a small, lightweight radio transmitter. With communications being such a vital asset in the desert, it was imperative for the soldiers to keep in contact with other units. However, units which had no radio used flag signals for short messages and for identification, especially in small tank units. Signalling with flags from tall buildings or high ground was the easiest and clearest way of transmitting information. Although visual signals were not used extensively in North Africa for transmitting various data, both sides used them.

BELOW: What appears to be an Allied tank has been knocked out of action. The extensive damage to this tank suggests that it may have caught fire and then exploded as its rounds, machine-gun ammunition, hand-grenades, and signal flares stowed on board detonated. By late 1942 most of the newly acquired British tanks were American-built Shermans and Grants, whilst only one-sixth of German-built tanks were the mighty PzKpfw IV. In late October the Germans had only 173 PzKpfw IIIs against 422 Grants and Shermans. For the PzKpfw IV, the total was 38 against 607 Crusaders, Stuarts and Valentines.

RIGHT Soldiers digging strong defensive positions prior to the British Operation 'Lightfoot' on 23 October 1942. Operation 'Lightfoot' was the start of the second, more famous battle at El Alamein, which would prove to be the major turning point for the *Afrika Korps*. The attack was launched by General Montgomery, and the main weight of these initial British thrusts came in the north and south. Resistance by the Germans was fierce and in some places British soldiers found the defences almost impregnable. This was no fault of their own; the Germans had become masters of defensive battle. Having learned these techniques on the Eastern Front, they were now using them across the arid desert of North Africa.

BELOW: Among the stones, a soldier lifts a dead gazelle – which he has just hunted and killed – by the horns. Fresh meat must have provided a welcome change for men who had grown tired of their normal, mundane rations in interminable tins. Even the captured British bully beef which the soldiers enjoyed could not beat a warm, freshly cooked piece of succulent meat. This soldier is armed with a 7.92mm (0.31in) Karabiner 98b (Kar). The length of the rifle was 1.25m (4ft 1in) and it weighed 4kg (8.8lb). With a muzzle velocity of 785m/s (2574ft/s), it was the most common German small arm issued in North Africa.

BELOW: An *Afrika Korps* soldier wearing a pith helmet, tropical shirt with matching shorts and ankle boots is collecting water, more than likely for the vehicle's radiator. His vehicle is a captured British Morris C8 4 x 4 'Quad' field artillery tractor that was primarily used for towing field guns and ammunition limbers. Troops were very careful at taking water from the wells they came across, as they knew the British were very clever at polluting waterholes, wells or distillation plants with deadly chemicals. However, special chemical processes normally purified any that had been contaminated. Every truck driver, soldier and officer was eagerly on the lookout for water; any damaged or dented water tanks which they found would be welded together to carry water. Although the *Afrika Korps* was accompanied by numerous water columns, the continuing strain on supplies to the front lines sometimes jeopardized the supply, affecting the men and the vehicles.

LEFT: With their pickaxes two well-tanned soldiers of the *Afrika Korps* are digging a pit for their tent. Their position has been well chosen, as it is protected by a rock face and avoids the full wrath of a desert storm. A sudden sand storm, a tearing wind, which drove sharp sand particles into faces and reduced visibility to less than 7m (23ft), made life hazardous out in the open desert. It was therefore imperative for soldiers to set up a tent with adequate shelter that would not only keep them warm from extreme night time temperatures, but could also be secured to the ground with sandbags in case a storm should suddenly blow up.

LEFT: Engineers extract water from a water hole. These wells were not the kind in which water bubbles out of the earth like a spring, but instead were normally found at a depth of many feet. Water was brought to the surface by pumps or other equipment. In this picture, the engineers are using a winch. Even during the retreat across the desert, the *Afrika Korps* still retained its numerous water columns, each equipped with a portable water pump that could be fitted with an overhead tank and tapping point, so that their vehicles and cans could be filled quickly after the pump had been erected. Various scouting units were sent out to look for spare parts that could be used in an emergency in order to erect such plants.

ABOVE: A signals battalion during a brief respite west of Alam El Halfa in September 1942. The soldiers are wearing the tropical *Feldmütze*, which is so bleached as to appear white against the contrasting colour of their dark-olive tunic. This was to be the furthest point of advance made by this signals battalion as the *Afrika Korps'* last hope of initiative in Africa had finally been lost. After the battle at El Alamein, Rommel was compelled to begin a long withdrawal across the desert. His army's retreat saved large numbers of the Axis army from destruction, and it only became a rout after Tripoli had fallen on 23 January 1943.

ABOVE: A rare chance to see a German supply column trying to reach stranded units that were coming under intensive enemy bombardment. This photograph was taken in March 1943, just a few weeks prior to the collapse of the African campaign. By this period the Allies ruled the sky and its armies massively outnumbered the Germans. With hardly any supplies getting through, the withdrawal in to Tunisia was an agonizing retreat for the soldiers. Whole divisions were now reduced to as few as ten tanks, and total troop strength across all divisions had fallen to an all-time low of only a few thousand men.

ABOVE: The long road back. A Horch Kfz 15 has become stuck in the sand in late November 1942. The driver tries to stop the vehicle's rear wheels from embedding even further into the sand by placing wooden boards under them. For some reason, this vehicle has been driven onto the beach and become stuck. The two officers on the left seem far from helpful and quite unconcerned about the event, despite the fact that by the end of 1942, the *Afrika Korps* was at a pitiful strength in materiel compared to its pursuers. For miles, numerous German Army vehicles could be seen stretched across the desert, either on tow because they had run out of fuel, or because they had developed some kind of mechanical failure and there was no time to fix them. In November 1942, Rommel took stock and, to his consternation, found he had only 21 tanks, 35 antitank guns, 65 pieces of field artillery, and 24 antiaircraft guns left to fight the huge might of Montgomery's Eighth Army. The end of Germany's *Blitzkrieg* campaigns had finally been decided in the deserts of North Africa.

ABOVE: On the back of a Opel-Blitz truck a 2cm (0.78in) Flak 30 light antiaircraft gun is being used as a support weapon on the ground. The smoke rising into the air is an indication that a heavier-calibre shell has probably hit the building. The 2cm Flak 30 gun weighed 463kg (1020lb). It had a muzzle velocity of 900m/s (2951ft/s) and boasted a maximum ceiling height of 2200m (2407yd). The weapon was very effective and had a rate of fire of 120–280 revolutions per minute. It was not just deadly against low-flying aircraft, but also against ground targets.

BELOW: With the use of scissor binoculars, this soldier is able to locate the movement of enemy positions for many miles without the prospect of being seen. All new defensive positions were thoroughly examined before erecting a new line. Reconnaissance took into account all enemy dispositions in the area and its capabilities. Through a series of patrols and intensive examination using observation with binoculars, the main centres of resistance could be easily located at points which were chosen for maximum effectiveness.

ABOVE: An *Afrika Korps* war grave is a visual reminder of the huge loss of life the campaign had inflicted. Each countless cross in the desert with its individual inscription bore witness to the victories and defeats, the death and injury, hunger and thirst of the campaign. These war graves marked the last resting places of those who had paid the supreme sacrifice for their country. By mid-April 1943 there had been such staggering losses inflicted on the *Afrika Korps* that Rommel's force had been reduced to holding a tight perimeter in the last range of hills which surrounded Bizerta and Tunis. With the prospect of surrender or total annihilation, a sick 'Desert Fox' returned to Germany to beg Hitler to allow the remnants of his gallant army to be evacuated. Hitler refused him point blank and told Rommel in no uncertain words there would be no surrender. He forbade Rommel the opportunity of returning, so that when the surrender did finally come he would not fall into enemy hands. A few weeks later on 12 May 1943 the *Afrika Korps* surrendered. General Cramer, the commander, sent out a last signal: 'Ammunition shot off. Arms and equipment destroyed. In accordance with orders received the *Afrika Korps* has fought itself to the condition of where it can fight no more. The German *Afrika Korps* must rise again.'

Index